Praise for *Storyt*

D1561684

"I have been privileged to call Sharo
heard so many stories from her over
you want to be entertained and also enlightened while you are laughing, crying, smiling, and sighing, then this is the book that is sure to do it! I can assure you that you won't be disappointed."

—Raymond Higby, MD, retired family physician and
addiction medicine practitioner

"From a pioneer whose work has shaped our understanding of disruptive dynamics within the family system and what must take place to heal them, comes a most welcome and timely book. Sharon Wegscheider-Cruse's *Storytelling Legacy* provides insightful and inspiring wisdom through the use of narrative and story and how a deepening awareness of our own personal stories can affect and shape our lives and create understanding and meaning over time."

—Dan Barmettler, founder and Director, The Institute for Integral Development, and former Co-Director of Conferences, US Journal Training

"Sharon has lived a rich and fulfilling life and her stories reflect that with humor, wisdom, and compassion. Her ongoing desire to help people continues to enrich their lives and inspire them to be their best selves. Read Sharon's stories and you'll be moved to ponder and write your own to great and lasting benefit."

—Susan Zimmerman, LMFT, author of *Rays of Hope:
Lighting the Way in Life's Transitions and Losses*

"Thanks to my adventurous aunts, I grew up with a love of storytelling. Our times together not only included reading books, but hearing stories from their own lives. Conversations were filled with tales of their mishaps, lessons learned, travels, and amusing people they met along the way. Whether consciously or not, they taught me that stories matter . . . and every life is filled with them." *Storytelling Legacy* is a great example. As Sharon Wegscheider-Cruse shares stories from her own life, she reminds us that we all have stories to tell. Don't keep them to yourself."

—Barbara Winter, author, speaker, and publisher

"Sharon Wegscheider-Cruse is a master storyteller. Her stories here feature equal helpings of wit, heart, and humor. She inspires and empowers readers to think about their own stories and share them with the world."

—**Jerry Moe, MA,** National Director of Children's Programs (retired),
Hazelden Betty Ford Foundation

"Sharon is a master storyteller who inspires, heals, educates, and loves those she touches with her writing. Her wisdom has been a lifeline to me. Sharing her life stories is a way to continue her legacy of love, joy, grief, and passions. You go, girl!

—**Cheryl Keller,** friend, confidante, and soul sister

"The latest book from Sharon Wegscheider-Cruse gives us permission and provides inspiration to speak the truth. For decades, Sharon's grace, grit, and gratitude has guided individuals and families to build bridges through their individual and collective stories. A force that has changed the trajectory of my life both personally and professionally, Sharon's stories have the power to heal, inspire, and most importantly, create action that can change our world."

—**Jill Krush,** CCO Choice House Treatment, Onsite Workshops guide,
therapist, trainer, psychodramatist, and fellow storyteller

"In *Storytelling Legacy*, Sharon tells it like it is—and she has had quite the life to share with us. With humor and tenderness, we walk through the author's experiences and feel an intimate connection to the 'story.' Featuring a cast of colorful characters, this is a most enjoyable and poignant read!"

—**Mel Pohl, MD, DFASAM,** Senior Medical Consultant,
Pain Recovery Program, The Pointe Malibu Recovery Center

"I have had the pleasure of knowing and working with Sharon for almost thirty years and thought I had heard most of her stories. Yet she seems to have an inexhaustible supply of wit and wisdom wrapped in anecdotes by turns affecting and amusing, and always instructive and inspiring."

—**Patrick Cotter,** writer and teacher on Canada's Wet Coast

"Sharon Wegscheider-Cruse's autobiographical *Storytelling Legacy* is a sumptuous smorgasbord of uplifting and often humorous stories about how and where she learned her valuable trove of lifesaving skills. She generously shares these with us as she models how vulnerability, courage, strength, and commitment to telling our own stories can help others find their own power and place in the world. She helped me change my life for the better. Sound interesting?"

—**Peter Alsop, PhD,** singer-songwriter, lecturer, grateful human

"In traditional cultures, it is an expectation and deemed essential, for the community's survival that the elders share the wisdom they have gathered over their lifetimes. Sharon's latest book is a 'must read' for those of us who want a guide to telling our own story. Imagine the gift of being able to sit at the knee of your ancestors as they shared their life lessons."

—**Ted Klontz PhD,** Associate Professor of Practice, Creighton University, Heider College of Business, Financial Psychology Institute

"Sharon's book contains insightful stories and observations that will allow you to reflect on your own life story and the lessons you want to pass on to others."

—**Melanie McNiff,** adventure-seeker, travel-loving millennial, and corporate consultant

"Sharon Wegscheider-Cruse has touched countless lives with her wise words and healing touch. Both professionally and personally, Sharon is a loved and loving sage and mentor.

During our forty-year friendship, Sharon has contributed mightily to our publishing and conference companies with multiple books and scores of presentations at professional conferences designed to provide hope and healing to individuals and families with childhood trauma wounds.

In this creative 'memoir' Sharon weaves a delightful treasure-trove of personal stories of a life well lived."

—**Gary Seidler,** co-founder, Health Communications, Inc., and US Journal Training

"Sharon Cruse has led an astonishing life—one of healing, teaching, learning, exploring and giving love and light to many thousands if not, indeed, millions. It is no wonder that on her amazing journey she has collected a bounty of stories, and as a gifted storyteller she has gathered a hundred of them to share with us. They run the gamut from tender and touching to funny and self-deprecating and are a joy to all who will be fortunate enough to read them."

—Doug Green, *Ranger Doug* and *Riders in the Sky*

"Sharon Wegscheider-Cruse has been one of the true pioneers in family treatment in the addictions field. When she began her work, few understood the traumatic impact of growing up or living with addiction. Today, family treatment has become common practice. I have known Sharon as a client, a colleague, a mentee, and a friend. Her work was a part of the jet fuel that helped to propel my own personal recovery. I owe her so much in my own personal life and in the family we have created, which is now three generations. Thank you, Sharon. I am a part of your story and you are part of mine."

—Tian Dayton, PhD, bestselling author, psychologist, and psychodramatist

"Our lives are measured by our stories. Story is the context of life, the meaning of life, the power of life, and the power of recovery. I grew up on Sharon's stories. As a mentor to me, Sharon has always known and honored the power of story, her story, and the story of others. Sharon is a master of the art of story. This book is a testament to the significance of story."

—Steven Earll, licensed professional counselor and
licensed addictions counselor in private practice specializing
in family trauma, addictions, codependency and recovery issues

"Sharon Wegscheider-Cruse is a trailblazer whose work, legacy, and impact on the recovery field speaks for itself. She is also a master storyteller and one of my favorite communicators. In Storytelling Legacy, she masterfully uses her wisdom and wit to inspire us through the art of storytelling. As she shares stories from her expansive career, she reminds us all that our own stories are important and worth sharing."

—Miles Adcox, Chairman, The Onsite Group,
and founder, Milestones Wellness Recovery Center

Storytelling
LEGACY
EVERYONE HAS STORIES

What Are Yours?

Sharon Wegscheider-Cruse

Health Communications, Inc.
Boca Raton, Florida

www.hcibooks.com

Library of Congress Cataloging-in-Publication Data
is available through the Library of Congress

© 2022 Sharon Wegscheider-Cruse

ISBN-13: 978-07573-2435-2 (Paperback)
ISBN-10: 07573-2435-5 (Paperback)
ISBN-13: 978-07573-2436-9 (ePub)
ISBN-10: 07573-2436-3 (ePub)

Publisher: Health Communications, Inc.
301 Crawford Blvd., Suite 200
Boca Raton, FL 33432-1653

Cover, interior design and formatting by Larissa Hise Henoch

I dedicate this book, first of all, to my late husband, Joe Cruse. We lived many of the stories together and the inspiration comes from keeping those memories alive.

I also dedicate this book to my family, relationships forged through storytelling as they listened to my stories over the years. They have given me ongoing support, love, and inspiration as we grew up together. My children, Patrick, Sandy, and Debbie, and my seven grandchildren have heard hundreds of stories and still encourage me to tell more. They are my major support team. Through emails and connection, they provide much of my inspiration and creativity. Without the constant computer, scanner, and printer help from my son Patrick, I would be stuck on the constant challenge of technology. My daughters provided me with warm knit shawls as I sat through many a cold night typing and Phil, my son-in-law, provided homemade food. It's been a family effort.

The same is true with my friends. The hours spent together, trips, and experiences all contributed to who I have become as a storyteller. Living near friends, I have tried these stories out with wonderful visits with each of my local friends, and you all know who you are. To go next door and always be greeted by an open door and a smile goes a long way toward feeling creative, heard, and inspired.

Lastly, I dedicate this book to you, the reader. May you remember your stories, and may you share them with those you love—of all generations. When all is said and done, we will leave the legacy of our willingness to tell our own stories. May you take your own trip down memory lane. Life begins and ends with a story.

"Owning our story and loving
ourselves through the process
is the bravest thing that
we will ever do."
—Brené Brown

Contents

Acknowledgments

This book would not be written without the vision and fore-sight of Peter Vegso, the publisher at Health Communications, Inc. (HCI). I was with another publishing house at the time I met him and already had a bestseller. However, when Peter and the cofounder of HCI and US Journal, Gary Seidler, came into my life, I started speaking and writing in a way that the public loved. Peter and Gary believed in me and my career as an author blossomed. More bestsellers followed with HCI. It's been a long, warm, and trusted relationship, and I've had the pleasure to work with so many kind and dedicated people there throughout the years. Working now with Christian Blonshine and my ever patient and devoted editor, Christine Belleris, makes inspiration, writing, and editing fun and fills my soul. Thank you also to Larissa Henoch, the talented art director who has crafted striking covers, illustrated eye-catching images, and designed beautiful interior designs for my books.

I thank my family, my greatest accomplishment, and to whom I am grateful for having a writing career. They have always been there for me and continue to support, love, and inspire me.

Thank you also to my friends—those special people I have connected with on a soul level, and those who provide some of the inspiration in this book. They have encouraged and supported my role as a storyteller. You know you are, and I won't include names because that would take another book.

Finally, I thank my Higher and Universal Power, whom I choose to call God.

Introduction

Storytelling is "prose to spark joy," and started to interest me when I was about twelve years old. While many kids might roll their eyes and make excuses when a relative started talking about something that happened to them in the past, I was enthralled, and the passion only grew from there.

By the time I was a teen, my first typewriter—the big, clunky, manual kind with the black, red and white ink ribbons—was my best friend. Stories about real people and places are far more dramatic than recited information, and they also carry messages. Learning to first tell and then write stories helped me know that we build connection by taking our raw personal data and make it come to life, conveying the culture, history, experiences and values that give a deeper understanding of the world in which we live.

My first writings as an author were long stories woven into original oratories. My first competitive piece was for a short story contest that ended up delivering as an oratory. I went to the top in my home state of Minnesota. To me, advocacy mattered, and storytelling was my vehicle. It has taken me to the point of publishing books, book-lets, speaking all over the world and loving my time with friends and family—still telling stories. Listening to others' stories is also a major part of my life. People often ask me, "Do you have hobbies you like to pursue?" My answer is that people are the most interesting focus I can have, so I "listen to" and "tell stories."

When I've shared my stories in groups and gatherings over the years, I'll often hear, "I think you should write up that story." It seems each time I heard that, the story had some kind of serendipity, coincidence, twist, or means to connect. That made my decision to write this book.

The group that really inspires me are those aged fifty-five-plus. When you've lived a long time, you've experienced so many changes on a global scale, and each of these events has informed our personal lives as well. Think about it—living through the Great Depression, wars, protests, the Civil Rights Movement, the Women's Movement, the use and abuse of illegal drugs, addiction recovery, splits in society and huge cultural inequalities, the explosion of technology, global climate change, the COVID-19 pandemic . . . I could go on and on, but you get the point.

Screens and data have overtaken our society; we are overloaded, digitalized, and distracted. Storytelling can be used to connect, engage, inspire, heal and create a brighter future. As storytellers, we experience the extraordinary power of sharing with others through our narratives of risk, surprise, adventure, joy, pain and someone who has "been there, done that" and have lived to tell about it. Give me a book—printed on real paper—and you have my interest. Tell me stories and you have me listening carefully. It's not nearly as much fun to snuggle with my iPad or Kindle.

I am an ordinary person who has had amazing and surprising events happen to me most of my life. I share them in the chapters of this book. I'm hoping to connect to you through them, and that they encourage you to share your own stories. In truth, we all have fascinating lives. Are you outgoing and fun-loving? You are a storyteller. Are you quiet and prefer to observe and watch the world go by? You are a storyteller. We are all storytellers, and we all benefit when we share our stories with one another.

Come along with me and let your own storytelling flourish.

"There is no friend as loyal as a book."
—Ernest Hemingway

"A good storyteller tells who, where, and why.
It takes us on a journey."
—Sharon Cruse

Chapter One
Celebrities

Inspiration by Barbara Bush

Many years ago, I was a guest speaker at The Phoenix, which at that time was an exclusive private club for upscale Houston, Texas, residents—including First Lady Barbara Bush. Looking out from my room at The Houstonian, I saw Barbara on a jogging path that circled the area, followed by two Secret Service agents. *Good for her,* I thought, and vowed to get out there and do the same sometime. Later that day, I surprised myself and attempted to do exactly that. I soon knew why I hadn't done this earlier. About a quarter of the way, I was winded and tired. I was much younger than she and, I assumed incorrectly, in better shape. That was an intervention for me.

A few months later, I went to Utah to the St. George National Institute on Fitness (NIF) and was confronted again with weakness, lack of stamina, and a few too many pounds. I was shocked when

I could not complete some entry exams. Then and there, I made a commitment to myself to truly get in shape. I couldn't even walk half a mile or manage a small incline without getting winded. My workaholism with a heavy travel schedule had left me too busy to exercise, and my enjoyment of great meals in exotic restaurants on expense accounts was my excuse for not eating well. It had all taken its toll on my health.

I made a resolution: I would go to NIF for a week each year and change my lifestyle. I would recheck annually until I could fairly easily walk five miles on an incline. And so began my lifestyle change. I walked every day. I took the time to meditate in the early morning. I stopped eating mindlessly in front of the television at night. I kept crocks of carrots and celery in our refrigerator for healthful snacking.

I kept my promise to myself, and I looked forward to my daily walking. I'd listen to Jerry Lee Lewis, Elvis Presley, and other types of rock 'n' roll music. I had routes in Las Vegas, the Black Hills of South Dakota, and Minnesota that fed my soul and happily wore out many pairs of walking shoes. I walk to this day—it's still my exercise of choice—with my routes in and around my home in Colorado. I've walked so much that I wouldn't be surprised if I've walked across the United States.

Little did Barbara Bush know what she inspired me to do on a business trip to Texas!

"Everything in life is within walking distance, if you have the time."
—Unknown

"Keep walking through the storm, your rainbow is waiting on the other side."
—Heather Stillufsen

Rocking Around the Clock
with Bill Haley and the Comets

My black Studebaker was my pride and joy. I had bought the car myself and outfitted it with Venetian blinds in the window and hot pink terry cloth seat covers. This was the 1950s, I loved driving around in it. When I heard Bill Haley and the Comets the first time on my car radio, I thought I had died and gone to heaven. I turned up the volume as I drove down Main Street, feeling like I owned the world whenever that song came on.

My hometown in southern Minnesota is a hundred miles from anywhere. Somewhere off the road in that hundred miles was another town called Sleepy Eye. It was like something you might find on the old television show *Little House on the Prairie*. The name of the town supposedly came from a Native American chief who had a sleepy eye. Sleepy Eye was popular with the local kids because it had a dance hall. We would head there on Saturdays and dance our hearts out. The weekly trip was often the highlight of our week.

One week, we arrived at the hall and were shocked to find a poster on the wall announcing that Bill Haley and the Comets were coming to play at the Sleepy Eye Dance Hall. You can imagine the hysteria. Could it really be true? Would this renowned group even be able to find this little town in southern Minnesota? It had to be true; after all, it was on a poster.

Everyone went into overdrive to get ready. People either bought new clothes or made something new. We polished our white bucks or ordered new ones. Dates were optional, but I did have one. I even let him borrow my car, because mine was way cooler than his. The big night came, and it wasn't just a dream—they were, indeed, there!

My date and I danced and sang the night away, whipping around the dance floor, my new twirl skirt lilting in the air. We all "rocked around the clock" until it was time to go home.

It was one of those magical nights when everything came together in a perfect way. We all have them: the excitement never fades, even all these years later.

"I really look for peak experiences and dramatic material that can allow peak experiences."
—Kathryn Bigelow

"Often, you never know the value of a moment until it becomes a memory."
—Debbie Carlille

Hoping for First Class Seats

My husband, Joe Cruse, had the honor and pleasure of planning and caddying in the Bob Hope Classic golf tournament. As you can imagine, it was a special time for all, particularly Joe who participated every year. He got to know Bob and his wife Delores, spending time on a Palm Springs, California, golf course with them. It was just plain fun. Joe took part for years, and I learned to watch golf. I never really enjoyed playing golf, but it made me happy to see Joe so happy.

At that time, travel was a big part of both of our personal and professional lives. Because we flew so much, we usually received first-class upgrades, which made all the traveling a little easier. We'd usually fly early in the morning, and enjoy a cup of coffee and breakfast, along with the morning newspaper. On one trip, we tried to get first class tickets but there were none available, and because of the time we needed to be at our destination to make it for a presentation that day, we needed to fly coach.

On the day of our flight, we boarded and were surprised to see no one sitting in first class, so asked the flight attendant if we could move forward. We had many miles and we had requested first class if there were any available seats. "No, I'm sorry," she said, "Someone will be boarding." Passengers continued to file in, and the plane filled, but none of them went to first class. Finally, everyone was buckled in, and the plane was ready to pull away from the gate when someone did board the flight and head for first class: Bob Hope. He was alone except for one bodyguard. He glanced back and saw Joe. They exchanged nods and smiles. Soon, to our delight, the flight attendant approached us and asked if we wanted to move forward. Apparently, Bob Hope had bought all of first class to assure his privacy, but he gladly welcomed us.

Joe and Bob talked and laughed nonstop, and I had an interesting flight seated next to the bodyguard. I learned a great deal about the behind-the-scenes work of keeping a celebrity safe. It was definitely a flight I'll never forget!

Gloria Steinem, Mr. T, and Me

When *The Larry King Show* called inviting me to be on the show and interviewed by the legendary journalist, I was delighted. I checked my schedule and accepted the invitation as a guest. The booker told me that I would share the hour with the actor Mr. T, who first gained fame for the television show *The A-Team* and his copious amounts of gold jewelry, and feminist activist and author Gloria Steinem. I was intrigued by how the show's producers arrived at this collection of guests!

I arrived at the Atlanta airport and was led by the greeter to a white stretch limo, which I had to myself. I noticed that there were two other white stretch limos that traveled with us. When I arrived at the CNN Center, where the show was filmed, I was ushered to the green room for a make-up and hair check. Mr. T was already there, and Gloria Steinem arrived shortly thereafter. We all shared the same story: we all had our "own" white limo. We conversed and got on quite well. I was a big fan of Ms. Steinem's and all that she had done for women's rights. I had to admit to Mr. T that I didn't know much about him, but I complemented him on his white suit and striking gold jewelry. Neither of them knew who I was. I filled them in, and we made a little more conversation before we walked out and took our places with Larry King.

Larry and I were about the same size, so we had high chairs. I noticed on the monitor that we all looked close to the same size when the show came on. He somehow made sense that we would all be there. Me, the Midwestern mother and wife who worked with addicts; Gloria the activist single woman; and an actor/wrestler, who really wasn't all that interested in either of us women but treated us like "ladies" and was a gentleman. King brought up a number of current issues and we all gave our viewpoints, sometimes we felt just the opposite about some of the subjects and sometimes we were all in agreement. Whatever the subject, whatever our answers, the phone lines lit up with questions for us all. It was a spirited and lively show and, when finished, Larry said, "Thank you. It was a good show."

Gloria called over the producer and said, "Let's not waste gas, drivers, and time. We can all go to the dining room together in the same limo." When we got to the hotel that CNN had provided for us, they had closed off one of the prime dining rooms for us, but they had set each of us up at our own table. Gloria took charge again and said, "Nonsense! Set the table up for three." It was an enlightening and fun evening. We shared dinner that night and discovered a lot about one another. We had much in common, even if it might not appear so on the surface, and got into lively but polite discussions about the things we did not. Some of the most interesting times in life are those that you never expect, and chance meetings with people you might otherwise never come to know.

"Expect the unexpected."
−Bear Bryant

"Unexpected events can set you back or set you up. It's all a matter of perspective....
−Mary Ann Rodmacher

Frogs and Wayne Newton

Every person reading this story will know what I am talking about. Women recognize bonding with other women while men support and sometimes shake their heads. Women innately know how to make girlfriends. I'm not sure what is happening in the world as you read this, but I would wager that the same kind of bonding (in some form) is taking place. Girlfriend bonding includes good food, deep and silly conversations, and much laughter, trust, pure joy, and connection. For me, many of those bonds have lasted a lifetime.

How many ways can we bond?
• Prom dresses or lack of prom dresses.
• Slumber parties.
• Clothes and shopping.
• Phone conversations—probably now texts and miscellaneous social media.
• Glass of wine.
• Boyfriend stories.

- Husband stories.
- Partner stories.
- Children stories.
- Grief and loss.
- Travel stories.

At one point in my life, there was a group of seven women who bonded. There are several reasons why we hit it off so well, but one was that we all had a deep faith and spiritual connection—not religious at all, only a universal belief in something greater. We named our individual belief as a God of each person's choice.

One night, at an adult slumber party, we were walking the Las Vegas Strip. After deciding we needed a mascot, we went into a toy store and each bought a plush toy frog. We chose the frog because of the acronym F – R – O – G - "Fully Relying on God."

We named ourselves "the Frogettes." That same night, we decided to go to the Wayne Newton show. We got front-row seats and were talking and laughing as the drums rolled and Newton's suspended high-in-the-air platform was lowered into the room. We each took out our frogs and put them on our shoulders, ready for Wayne to take the stage. He landed, and his eye caught sight of the seven women with frogs on their shoulders—how could he miss us? He walked over to us, and then said, "Are those frogs—and why?" We told him our story and he dedicated his next song, "I Did It My Way" to "the Table of Women and their Frogs."

For many years, we Frogettes had an annual meeting in Las Vegas. Later on, you'll meet the Giraffettes.

"Your circle of friends must match your aspirations, dreams, and values—or you will find little support when you need it."
—Anonymous

Johnny Cash and June Carter Cash

My husband Joe had a contract with a professional baseball team, and we happened to be in Tennessee for business at their annual camp. While there, Joe received a call and both he and I were invited to come to Vanderbilt Hospital and meet someone who wanted to meet both of us.

The call was from country star June Carter Cash, and she asked us to come visit her husband Johnny Cash, who was in the hospital. We went, of course. The meeting itself was very interesting. June told us how important it was to be discreet and to slide into the hospital and not give any indication that we were coming to meet her. Joe and I dressed as inconspicuously as possible and tried our best to be discreet and nonchalant as we entered the building. June, however, was not dressed quite as inconspicuously. She greeted us wearing a floor-length sable coat and was flanked on each side by a bodyguard. She was a striking beauty. It all went from there. That meeting was the start of a great friendship with the Cashes.

They invited us to their home in Hendersonville, Tennessee. It was a beautiful home and as June showed us around, their personalities came forward in the various rooms. John's room was black, with guitars hanging on the walls. Music was everywhere in this home, as you'd expect. June's bedroom was filled with beautiful clothes, including a rack of mink coats. I treasured her black mink. Little did I know that Joe had bought it on the spot, and it still hangs in my closet. Their kitchen was my favorite room in their house, maybe because it felt so genuine. It is where June canned tomatoes and made her own jelly.

She was a great cook and Johnny adored her. It didn't surprise me that Johnny died shortly after losing June. He so loved her.

I was a longtime Johnny Cash fan, so this whole time was a thrill for me. They were good people. We also got to know Johnny's daughter Rosanne Cash. John accepted Joe's invite and came to the Betty Ford Center and gave an April Easter Sunday concert. Joe flew to Nashville and brought Johnny to the dessert. It was a thrilling night and I still have the poster in my apartment.

Johnny and June enriched our lives and their music and friendship still live in my heart.

> **"Not all heroes and heroines wear capes.**
> **Two of mine sang; one played guitar and**
> **the other played the autoharp."**
> —Sharon Cruse

Johnny Cash and the Hell's Angels

My mother was a fun-loving risk-taker, but never did I think I would find her mixing it up with an American icon and the world's most notorious motorcycle gangs. Let me backtrack a bit. Her favorite entertainer, Johnny Cash, was coming to Rapid City, South Dakota, near where she lived. She didn't have much money to spare, particularly for something like a concert, but my brother surprised her by saying that he had bought tickets for the two of them to attend the concert. He would drive the many miles to see that she got there. The show was nearly sold out and while my mother was thrilled to be there, she was disappointed to discover that their seats were near the top row of a big theater, and she could barely see Johnny who looked like a little spec.

About a half hour into the show, Mom excused herself and told my brother she was going to the bathroom. He trusted that she could find one since there are many in the Rapid City Civic Center. After a while, he realized she had been gone a long time, but he had no way of knowing which bathroom she had gone to.

All of the sudden, there was a big commotion near the stage. The Hell's Angels motorcycle gang had come into the theater and were threatening to disrupt the show. Johnny Cash wasn't rattled at all. Rather than calling for help, he just kept singing and then invited the gang to come sit on the edge of the stage and enjoy the show up close and personal. They did just that and guess who was with them? My mother! Despite their reputation, they helped this older lady get up on the stage and she, too, enjoyed Johnny Cash—up close and personal.

So how did this happen? Mom really wasn't going to the restroom. She decided she was going to find a closer seat when she ran into the Hell's Angels and just decided to follow them. Surprisingly, they didn't stop her and then they invited my mom to join their group as they moved their way to the front of the house. This story will forever live in our family lore!

This was long before I became a friend of Johnny's, whom I met after she had passed. She would have been thrilled. I told him about this later, of course, we laughed about it, and he said he was sorry my mother wasn't alive after we'd gotten to know each other, or he would've contacted her. He was that kind of guy. Life, as they say, is often more interesting than fiction.

"The Hell's Angels try not to do anything halfway,
and anyone who deals in extremes are bound to cause
trouble, whether he means to or not. This, along with a
belief in total retaliation for any offense or insult, is what
makes the Hell's Angel 's unmanageable for the police
and morbidly fascinating to the general public."
—Hunter S. Thompson

Michael Landon: Larger than Life

Most people knew actor Michael Landon as Charles Ingalls on
the television show *Little House on the Prairie,* and as Little Joe Cart-
wright on *Bonanza.* He was so dashing as he rode around on his
horse. In real life, he knew my husband, and Joe introduced me to him
at a celebrity auction in Los Angeles. I expected him to be tall—he
was such a commanding presence on screen—but I was surprised to
find that he wasn't much taller than I was—about five foot nine inches
tall. We had a very good visit, and Joe and I ended up buying some of
the dishes he donated to the auction. Every once in a while, I still have
a meal on them. Despite his physical stature, to me he was six feet tall,
ever the robust man I had come to know on screen. He was incredibly
handsome, and his beautiful hair added an inch or so. Michael shared
with us later, in private, that he wore four-inch lifts in his boots, rode
smaller horses just for the show, and stayed on the horse as much as
he could. Rarely was he filmed next to someone tall. Check it out the
next time you see one of these shows on reruns on one of the nostalgia
channels! Michael's fans loved him. Joe and I did as well.

Screens have the way to deceive. Often, when I would make an
appearance at a conference, people would come up to meet me and
say, "You are so small, I expected you to be much taller." I realized

eventually that many of the audiences had met me through film or on a stage. I usually was elevated in those early encounters and so I looked much taller. I would walk along the stage in my high heels, shaking hands and looking tall. When I was right next to people in a workshop, they discovered that I was nowhere near the statuesque woman that they expected. Although they were incredibly uncomfortable, I always worked in three- and four-inch heels—even running around airport terminals in them. When I turned fifty, I gave myself the gift of telling myself that I had to never wear high heels again. And I didn't. I am a real boot girl. Age has taken its toll as well. When people ask me how tall I am, my answer is—then or now? The truth is, besides just losing the shoes, we all lose height as we age. But what I've come to learn is that it really doesn't matter!

**"A person's a person,
no matter how small."**
—Dr. Seuss

**"Even the smallest person can
change the course of the future."**
—J. R. R. Tolkien

Call from the White House, President Gerry Ford

I was enjoying breakfast one morning when I lived in Las Vegas when the phone rang. This was before Caller ID, when you had to actually answer the phone to know who was on the other end. If we'd had Caller ID, I probably would have run when it rang. The caller simply said, "Good morning. This is the White House."

Surprised, and just to make sure I heard correctly, I said, "Who is calling?"

"I am calling for Betty Ford, who is inviting you to come to Washington, DC, to attend the funeral of her husband, President Gerald Ford. Would you like the details?"

"I'm so sorry to hear this news," I responded, and added, "Yes, I'd like the details, please."

"Be in Washington in forty-eight hours and check into the Mayflower Hotel where all information about your stay will be waiting at the desk. Everything will be arranged, and everything is taken care of (hotel, meals, transportation, etc.). You only need to tell me, in this call, if you will be in attendance."

I'd passed this on to Joe, who was sipping coffee and reading the paper. He signaled "yes," and we were on our way. Many times in life, a split-second response is called for and this was one of those. Needless to say, we had to rearrange our schedules—stopping, cancelling, and rearranging events. After a few hours, our plans were finalized, and our tickets were at the airport waiting for us when we arrived. We flew commercial first class to the nation's capital where we were met at the airport. The rest of our agenda was waiting at the Mayflower. The next few days unfolded and we walked through it all.

We saw and met the other living presidents and their wives, we sat with Larry King, a photo of us sitting in the National Cathedral is still in the news archives. It all started with that one phone call.

The pageantry, the respect, the honor and the glory of it all was a highlight for both of us. We entered five days of an unforgettable experience. It was very sobering and also sad. I had come to know President Ford as we rode around in limos together. He was a kind, gentle, very wise, compassionate soul and I treasured knowing him as a man, as a husband, and as a President. There is no politics involved with the goodness of the soul. He had this goodness as a human being. I am humbled to this day for having had this experience.

"History and experience tell us that moral progress comes not in comfortable times, but out of trial and confusion."
–President Gerald Ford.

Jimmy Carter and My Son

Mothers have to learn to let go—over and over again. As the thread runs through this book, my life and politics have co-existed for many years. Perhaps the start, for me, was coming of age in the 1950s, when Eisenhower jackets were popular. We all wore them in my social group. Learning more about Ike the person, and his policies, I decided he would be the first president I voted for. Later on, as my education included more than just fashion, politics became very important to me. Going back to college as an adult in the 1960s cemented my deep interest in politics. I became a fan of Jimmy Carter and the whole-someness and unpretentiousness he brought to the office.

When my then sixteen-year-old son announced he wanted to go with a group to New York and attend a Jimmy Carter campaign rally, I said, "No, you are not traveling from Minneapolis, Minnesota, with people I don't know to attend a rally. He was very disappointed. I knew that he had his heart set on going, but to let my teenage son take off in a van with people I didn't know, to travel to a major city he didn't know, and live on a shoestring did not feel safe, wise, or responsible. The situation hung in the air for a few days.

He came to me later armed with a different argument in support of why I should let him go. He asked me to

remember my younger days and how I talked about civic responsibility. He asked me to look at the way I lived—a bit unconvention-
ally—and remember why I protested in 1960s. He made good points
that I took to heart, and I decided this would be the first of many
"letting go" times. Mind you, this was before cell phones and instant
communication. It was a true "letting go."

I drove him to the spot where the van would pick him up, and
waved good-bye. Waiting until the van was out of sight, the tears
flowed easily. My daily prayers were with and for him. He took a very
important step in forming his civic and worldview, and his passion
for politics, while I took a step in the direction of truly learning to
trust him and let go.

When he returned, he enthusiastically told me stories about the
great speeches he'd heard, and how excited he was to meet Amy
Carter, Jimmy's daughter. To this day, we still talk about this eye-
opening event that was so life-changing for him.

Today, we often have political discussions and share a passion for
doing good, for taking positive action, and committing to ideas and
values. We probably talk politics more than many mothers and sons.
It all started with a leap of faith and letting go.

**"Some believe holding on and hanging in there are signs
of great strength. However, there are times when it takes
much strength to know when to let go and then do it."**
—Ann Landers

Breakfast with George W. Bush

The chairman of the board of my company was George W. Bush's
roommate in college, and they remained good friends. When Bush
was running for his second term as president, he was scheduled to

attend a prayer and fundraising breakfast in Minnesota. Although my board chairman had donated to the campaign and had purchased a table for the event for a substantial amount of money, he couldn't attend. He asked me to please attend in his place. I was already booked into a conference, and it was going to be hard for me to attend the breakfast and still meet my commitment, but I said I would. Somehow, one knows when to say "yes" and when to say, "I can't."

I was off to an early start the day of the breakfast, which began at 6:30 AM. Just getting there was an ordeal because of morning traffic and parking problems at the hotel. However, I made it on time, and received a message (delivered in person from the front desk—remember, no cell phones back then) from my chairman making sure I was there. I was at the table in his place, and I assured him that all was well—just as he wanted it to be.

President Bush was late arriving, and he had a great deal to say. The hotel delivered a second message from my chairman to make sure all was still well and that I was getting on well with First Lady Barbara Bush. She and I had met previously at The Phoenix Spa in Houston and rekindled our acquaintance. Even though it I was enjoying myself, the fact remained that there were seventy-five people in another audience in a different hotel waiting for me to show up on time and deliver a lecture that they had paid for. There was no way I could stay until the end of this event. I had to leave immediately, and, if everything went smoothly, I'd still barely make it in time.

I said good-bye to Barbara, got up, and slithered away as quietly as I could just as President Bush finished speaking and the ballroom filled with a sea of red, white and blue balloons dropped from the ceiling. At the same time, reporters and television cameras covering the event, focused in on the lectern and the front table—including me trying to make my stealthy exit. On both the six o'clock and the ten o'clock news that night was a clear shot of yours truly with the words, "Someone didn't wait for President Bush to finish" splashed across the screen as I crouched and tiptoed out the door. Fortunately, my chairman understood my predicament and actually thought it was funny. More importantly, so did President Bush!

> **"I heard an airplane passing overhead.**
> **I wished I were on it."**
> —Charles Bukowski

Presidents Are People, Too

Growing up, I never would have expected to meet and get to know not just one, but a few United States Presidents. I probably never would have if not for my husband, Joe Cruse.

Joe met Dwight Eisenhower when Joe was chief of staff at Eisenhower Hospital in Palm Desert, California. Joe spent time with Ike when he was in the hospital, and they had good chats.

We also got to know Gerald Ford. Betty Ford and Joe traveled extensively because of Joe's involvement with The Betty Ford Center as its medical director. Thus, President Ford and I spent much time together as the "spouses of the people on the program." This was when I learned all about how the Secret Service worked . More than once, I behaved in such a way that I felt their hand on mine to stop me. Things like opening a door, getting up to go to the bathroom without security, riding in the back of limos while Joe and Betty got the front seats. I liked President Ford and I think he enjoyed me. We had many good talks. Neither of us was used to being second fiddle and we both rather enjoyed the role. Less pressure.

George H. W. Bush was an advocate for The Betty Ford Center and came to the desert to speak at its opening. He was so supportive of Joe as its medical director and many of the presidents had quiet connections to the desert, to the Eisenhower Medical Center and Joe became friends of several of them.

Joe also introduced me to Ronald Reagan, who was a personal friend of someone my husband had dated, long before we were married. Both Ronald and Joe were a little awed to meet each other because they both shared the same friend and she had talked about each of them to the other; she had bult them both up. Joe tells the story of how the first time they met, they both kept nodding heads because they didn't know what to say to each other; they both felt a little awkward, and it was some time before they found meaningful conversation.

Joe and I were longtime patients at the Mayo Clinic, in Rochester, Minnesota. One morning, we arrived to have our blood drawn there. As we moved from our hotel through the tunnels and halls leading to the blood clinic, we were surprised to discover them empty. This was a Monday morning, when there are usually hundreds of blood draws conducted. We soon found out why when we saw the only other patients there: President Reagan and First Lady Nancy Reagan. They were as shocked as we were. Apparently, the tunnels had been closed for security purposes, but somehow Joe and I got through. After the surprise wore off, the four of us had a good visit.

Presidents are powerful, but they are also people. It was the entourage around them that was hard to handle, controlling (as they need to be) that was harder to work with. I'm still awed that we knew several presidents.

**"Leaders become great not because of their power,
but because of their ability to empower others."**
–John Maxwell

Garrison Keillor and Lake Wobegon

I was born and raised in Minnesota. Once a Minnesotan, always a Minnesotan. Sharing those Minnesota roots with humorist Garrison Keillor has always been a sense of pride. I became a fan that first time I heard Keillor broadcast his hilarious Lake Wobegon stories on the radio. My dial was always set to hear his latest broadcast and then, which I could, I attended his live shows. He managed to capture the thrill of canning tomatoes, listening to the birds, and ruminating with friends—connecting him to me and to all in the Lutheran parts of the country. He aptly captured the stoicism of Minnesotans with his lighthearted show that captured the hearts of people around the country. For instance, one of my stoic Minnesota friends once commented, "I loved my wife so much, I came close in those thirty years, to almost telling her."

How I love the "Minnnnesoooota" feelings I get when I meet other natives of my home state. Ice fishing, cabins up north, planting and harvesting gardens, and always having homemade jellies, jams, and veggies readily handy was a way of life. Coming from the city and approaching the limits of town, would simply start the cravings. I remember calling my aunt one day as I was getting close to her farmhouse. I told her that Joe and I were about two hours away and would come take her to the best restaurant in town; she laughed. Two hours later, we turned on the road to the farmhouse. The car windows were rolled down on the warm day, and immediately the vehicle was filled with captivating smells from her kitchen. Walking in, we found a pork roast just finishing up in the oven, a baked apple pie cooling (made with apples from her trees), whipped potatoes in a warming dish, fresh salad made with bounty from her garden, and biscuits browning. Going to Aunt Laurie's house was a culinary treat hard to find in any restaurant.

Garrison Keillor has the ability to capture these Minnesota minutes in his work—whether it be a live show or radio broadcast of "A Prairie Home Companion," or a podcast. He feels them, then captures them and has the ability to share them like no one else does. Topping off his sharing with red socks, a deep voice and a love of the Midwest all contributes to his role as a Minnesota icon—something to cherish.

Once I was driving through a little Minnesota town that I didn't know existed. It felt exactly what I imagined Lake Woebegone of Garrison Keillor fame would look like. It was small (about 500 people) and had a two-block long Main Street. The sight of lilac trees, lush green grass, and a stream running through it spoke to my soul. After we were nearly eight miles down the road, I said to Joe, "Go back please. I saw a 'For Sale' sign on a house and I want to buy it." He turned the car around and later that day, we owned a house in Marine on St. Croix, Minnesota. It was only later that we found out that Garrison Keillor was living there. Our local grocery store, complete with a meat market and bakery shop in the basement certainly could have been the inspiration for Ralph's Pretty Good Grocery Store. For eight years we spent our summers in Marine on St. Croix, and it was a treasured part of our lives. We have cemetery plots in the local cemetery and will go back and share part of eternity in this beautiful little town, as Garrison Keillor said when ending his shows "where the women are strong, all the men are good-looking, and the children are above average."

"You get older, and you realize there are no answers, just stories."
–Garrison Keillor

Red Skelton: Giving Us the
Gift of Art and Laughter

In the early days of television, there were only a handful of channels to watch, and variety shows were very popular. It was a different era in history and entertainment, and families would gather together to watch the latest live event on their black-and-white screen. It seems so long ago, but memories bring back the joy and feeling of belonging that was a part of that time. A mainstay of the era was *The Red Skelton Show*, headlined by the great comedian who brought the antics of characters Clyde Clemcadellehopper and Freddie the Freeloader into our living rooms and made us laugh until we cried. Red Skelton had a way of making these fictional characters come alive as we all waited for their weekly antics. Families had so much fun together.

On stage, Red Skeleton was full of humor and had the ability to maintain a twenty-year run on CBS and NBC. He was the son of a cleaning lady and a grocer; his story made was made up of a colorful history of vaudeville, burlesque, and simply making people laugh. His talent was natural and his role as a clown set the standard.

Sadly, the saying, "laughing on the outside and crying on the inside" was a true story for Skeleton. His son was only nine years old when he was diagnosed with an aggressive form of leukemia. Tragically, he died within a year of diagnosis. Truly, behind the laughter and joy Skeleton brought to this world, was a man who knew about personal pain. His wife, Georgia, knew my husband and she had several professional sessions with him.

When Georgia came to Joe's office, Red would sit in the waiting room and do sketches of clowns. He would usually have it finished by the time the session was over. He would give these good-size sketches to whomever else was sharing the waiting room with him. The recipients were surprised when he simply signed them and gave them away. I wasn't one of those recipients, but I do have Skelton's book, *Gertrude and Heathcliffe,* autographed to Joe in memory of the good times.

Tragedy continued for Red when Georgia died by suicide. Red Skeleton was a good and kind man, dealing with loss and grief by accepting his talents. In many ways, his lessons still teach us all, that sometimes laughter is the best medicine.

His shows are still available on YouTube. Take a look and let them life your spirits.

"Live by this credo: have a little laugh at life and look around you for happiness instead of sadness. Laughter has always brought me out of unhappy situations."
—Red Skelton

Virginia Satir: A Powerhouse Woman Who Changed My Life

Virginia Satir was a powerhouse of a woman. She was the founder of experiential family therapy, and she changed the lives of thousands and thousands of people. I first heard about her before the Internet, before cell phones, before Google or Wikipedia. Someone gave me a handout when I was in college with her stated beliefs about family systems. This was before she had even published her signature book *Peoplemaking.* Those two pages helped me make a few lifechanging decisions, and I was determined to meet her. I tried everything but couldn't find her. Knowing there had to be a way, I started my first center using those two sheets of paper and the knowledge and concepts that I gleaned from her.

At the time, I was teaching at the University of Minnesota in Public Health. Many nights, I drove home on snow-covered streets. One of those nights, I had a tire on my car blow out. Feeling stranded, alone, in the dark, I felt powerlessness. I grabbed a flashlight and walked through the streets until I found a house with a shoveled driveway and lights on inside. I walked up and knocked on the door. A man answered the door, and his wife was beside him. After explaining my plight, they invited me in.

They kindly gave me hot chocolate and then offered to help change my tire. As we talked more, they shared they were leaving at the end of the week to go to Canada to study with Virginia Satir. After registering shock, I said, "I have been trying to find her for two years. How can I go?" They explained there was no way that I would be able to attend because it was government sponsored and only for Canadian citizens. They had dual citizenship and so they could go. That was not good enough for me. I took the phone number for the event and began my "begging calls" to the workshop organizers. They said "no" on the first seventeen calls I made that week. On the eighteenth call, they probably knew that I would just keep asking, so they said "come." I would've gladly paid, but there wasn't a registration fee, and they wouldn't be able to charge me. A week later, I was on an airplane heading to Canada.

I saw her sitting in a booth at the hotel before the conference started. I recognized her from the photo on the brochure. I walked over and said, "I don't mean to interrupt, but . . .".

She looked up and said, "You already have interrupted me, now sit down and let's talk."

This event and that conversation changed the course of my life.

**"I want to love you without clutching . . . appreciate you
without judging . . . join you without invading . . .
criticize you without guilt . . . and help you without insulting.
If I can have the same from you, then we can
truly meet and enrich each other.**
—Virginia Satir

Sophia Loren and the Last Laugh

Joe and I rarely disagreed about things. However, there was one way in which we were different. To Joe, a conference meant meetings, continuing education credits or medical license credits and for sure, lots of doctor friends and time to visit, share coffee, and talk "medical things."

To me, conferences meant usually presenting a lecture or workshop, good meals, fatigue, and falling into a comfortable hotel bed after a long day. Sometimes, there was also a time-consuming book autographing session. One such was conference was the book publishing trade show in Chicago. We were both looking forward to the trip for different reasons. Being a very independent woman, I often went to conferences alone though sometimes Joe would go as well. For some reason I don't remember now, I wanted him to stay right with me. We had each made a presentation, but I had a current book release and there was going to be a long, extended book-signing time. I asked Joe to stay with me. Maybe bring me a cup of coffee or a Diet Coke, maybe a bottle of water, and just some company as the day dragged on. He said, "Sure, I will be with you." An hour later, one of his colleagues from Palm Springs came over and invited Joe to coffee in the bistro to talk over the latest "who knows what." He jumped at the chance and said, Sorry, honey, you know I haven't seen Charlie for quite a while, and you will be just fine." Many days that would be true, but this wasn't one of them.

I headed for the book-signing table, while Joe went to meet his friend, and prepared for another hour. As staff walked me to the front of the line of people eagerly holding their books, I caught a glimpse of who my neighbor would be in the author area. Sitting at the table right next to me was actress Sophia Loren! I let her know immediately that I was delighted to share this space next to her and we started to chat. She is stunningly beautiful in person and wore a dazzling jeweled necklace. It was hard to decide what was more beautiful: her complexion, her hair, her eyes, her warm smile, or that amazing emerald necklace. She had written a new cookbook that she was debuting at this convention. We visited for the hour of signing and I couldn't wait to meet Joe later and tell him all about my encounter.

He listened painfully as I buzzed with excitement. His friend was boring, and Joe left early. He thought about coming to the signing area but didn't want to work his way through the lines. So, he read the first edition of the "Dummies" books. He said it was appropriate because he felt like one when he realized what he had missed!

> **"I would much rather eat pasta and**
> **drink wine than be a size 0."**
> —Sophia Loren

White Eagle: Peak Moment

A special peak moment in my life was being invited to speak at a major church in California, with several thousand people in attendance. It was beautiful, with flowers, light, and a full orchestra playing.

How many hundreds of times had I given this same presentation, but in church basements and town halls and schools all over the country? Now, looking out at this huge audience was certainly powerful, yet I recognized the same thrill I felt in cramped church basements when someone was about to make sense of their family system.

A year earlier, living in Rapid City, South Dakota, I had already been introduced to a delightful Native American man who had grown up on a reservation and taught himself to sing opera. He and his pianist, David Strickland, were two of the finest and most talented musicians I had ever heard. I was moved deeply and spiritually by their music. It was a peak moment to share a stage with both of them. White Eagle was the guest singer and David Strickland was the pianist and listening to them was a mystical experience. Imagine my thrill as White Eagle came on stage to introduce me to the crowd as his friend from South Dakota. The power of his presentation seared into the hearts and souls of everyone in that building, including me. It was a peak moment I will never forget.

Me, from a town of 500 in southern Minnesota and White Eagle, growing up on the reservation in South Dakota. The fact we shared a stage together with 10,000 people waiting to hear his music and my thoughts on families and addictions. One has to believe in the power bigger than any of us to have orchestrated that happening. It was a peak moment, for sure.

**"You are not a pawn in the chess game of life,
you are the mover of the pieces."**
—White Eagle

> "

Chapter Two
Cultural Stories

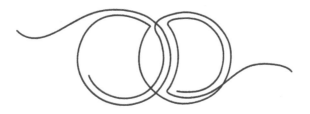

Caste Systems and My Hometown

When you hear the term caste systems, most people would think about South Asia or ancient cultures. Traditionally, a caste system is a class structure that is determined by birth—one from which it is impossible to move up. But are caste systems with us—no matter who we are or where we came from?

In a very general manner, many of these stratifications begin with our family. If you are born into wealth, you have more opportunities than someone born into poverty. Even more loosely, it can also mean who lives where. Some caste systems depend on culture, some on religion, and some on geography. Some believe it has to do with karma (the work you do and the choices you make) and others believe it has to do with dharma (the nature of reality).

In my hometown, there were several stratifications. There were those who lived on farms and those who lived in town. There were also divisions by religions. My town was Comfrey, Minnesota, in the southern part of the state. It supported and was supported by the farms that surrounded it. There were town people and farm people. We had different lifestyles and our connecting points were the town schools, the two-block long shopping area, and the churches. Everyone knew everyone and about everyone. There are very few secrets in a town this size. When someone died, one of the churches rang its bell for the age of the person who died, and you usually knew who it was. At noon, the town whistle blew, and you knew it was time to eat lunch. Farmers had to depend on one of two things happening: either someone brought you lunch, or you went hungry. There was no leaving the work.

Further division in the system was what you believed. You probably didn't know the whole story, but you usually followed whatever your parents did. It was the way of things back then. Our town had eight churches. This is quite a few when the total population of our town was 546—and the number changed when anyone moved in or out or died. Seven churches were some sort of Lutheran (German, Swedish, Norwegian, and so forth) and one –the largest one—was Catholic. If you married anyone from a different church, even though it was still Christian, it was called a "mixed marriage" and people showed concern and prayed it would "turn out."

Because of our tight connections through churches and occupation, all the people born outside of the city limit, on the western side, were residents of Liberty Park. It only meant that you weren't a Comfreyite. The only connection most of us had to Liberty Park was to let their children use our schools. We had a public grade school and a Catholic grade school, and we all shared the same high school. As I grew up and learned about the caste systems of India, parts of South Asia, and Sri Lanka, I understood. After all, I was a Comfreyite.

"Bloom where you are planted"
−1 Corinthians 7:20–24

What Are You Going to Do?

These words echoed in my mind today hearing that my good friend, Sam, had died last night. Whenever Sam heard my tales of woe or when he shared that he had a woe of his own, he would put his hands in the air and exclaim, "What are you going to do?" He told me he had done that often in life. Sam was remarkable and his friendship was a gift.

Sam had not had an easy life. He was a Holocaust survivor as was his wife, Angela. We lived next to each other for about twenty years. In the beginning, we talked on some occasions about the Holocaust. The obvious sign they were Holocaust survivors were the numbers tattooed on both their arms. Little by little, they shared more and more.

They shared how Sam was in Buchenwald and described the horrific, brutal conditions there—truly the deepest levels of man's inhumanity to man as Sam witnessed countless beatings and tortures. He was able to escape the worst of the conditions by the mere fact that he was a good painter. He had lived humbly as a decorator painter apprentice as a young boy. He was in his early twenties when he was sent to the camp.

At sixteen, Angela was a good seamstress—both by hand and on machines. She told the story of her father (and her whole family) being taken from her father's shop and sent to Auschwitz. Later, she and her family were corralled for the trip that went to the cremation ovens. They were being loaded into train boxcars, though her box-car was getting full, so they pulled fourteen members of her family (mother, father, uncles, grandparents and the rest of the children) out of line. She watched in horror as, one by one, as each was shot. She was loaded onto the train and the train left. She and Sam met in that boxcar.

Just before getting to the oven site, the train stopped, and they pulled off about ten people. Each was told why. Angela had been saved because she was useful as a seamstress and Sam was saved for his talents as a painter. This was their fate until the time of liberation. It so happened that my dad was in the army group that helped in the liberation, and I have his scrapbook of photos. I shared them with Sam and Angela, and we all cried together.

My dad had been serving in Germany for almost four years, and he had seen much pain and destruction. However, as he helped liberate Dachau, he saw unspeakable horror and man's inhumanity to man: cremation ovens, abandoned children and families, death and more death. He was a changed man and the memories of this time stayed with him forever

When I asked Sam how he survived it all, up went his hands and he said what he always did, "What are you going to do?"

Same was one of the kindest, most loveable, gentlest, and wisest persons I have ever met. He died last night—at 101 years of age and left very big footprints on my heart.

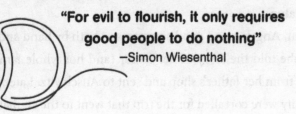

"For evil to flourish, it only requires good people to do nothing"
—Simon Wiesenthal

My Desire to Be a Priest

From my earliest years in grade school, becoming a priest was my quest. The sermons on Sunday excited me; so many possibilities and so much to learn. My education was coming from Notre Dame nuns teaching at a small Catholic School in Comfrey, Minnesota. They seemed to know more than I did, but nothing I was learning was as exciting as when the priest walked to the lectern and shared his message. Becoming a nun might have seemed more appropriate a goal for me at the time, but their role wasn't nearly as exciting as the priests' was. For one, all the nuns all looked the same to me, like little penguins, with their black-and-white habits with the white biblike insert on the front. They'd glide around the rooms with their arms folded in front of them. Priests, on the other hand, entered the area in silk robes, colorful and swishing, with braids and decorations. They commanded attention.

The nuns used books and papers and their lessons felt structured and boring. Sister Lucy was the principal. She brought out my fear and anger as she disciplined the boys by using a strap and the girls by hitting their hands with a ruler. Behind her back, we called her Sister Lucifer. I didn't have to experience her until I was in sixth, seventh, and eighth grade. My middle school teacher, grades four and five, was Sister Peony; she was sweet and kind—just like the flower that was her namesake. Sister Beatrice was my third-grade teacher. First and second grade were in another town in a one-room school (all eight grades in one room!).

What I wanted for myself was an important sounding name to respect like Father Peter Berger, Father Eugene Burke II or Father Mark Dealand. They were so much more impactful. My burning desire was to wear the robes, enjoy the colors, and find the forum to speak. Original oratory seemed so much more meaningful than the written word.

When meeting the resistance of the hierarchy of the rules of the church, having to accept that all the apostles were men, hearing it was a man that saved the world, and facing the word no, so many times in my quest to become a priest, I finally had to accept that there was no path to become a priest at that time. It is different now. I attempted, futilely, to at least become an altar girl, which was also rebuffed, and so my suspicions grew about the control of the male hierarchy. Later in life, this internal resistance shaped many of my spiritual decisions, and it never helped to hear "Well, you could have become a nun!"

I think it only makes sense to seek out and identify structures of authority, hierarchy, and dominion in every aspect of life and to challenge them; unless a justification for them can be given.
—Noam Chomsky

Guaranteed Growth at the Esalen Institute

The Human Potential Movement of the 1970s drew me in early and I stayed late. The mecca of great thinkers and leaders at that time was the Esalen Institute in Big Sur, California. It was the place to meet the greats in our field. During my time there, Esalen had workshops with Fritz Perls, Virginia Satir, Dick Price and Michael Murphy. One day, the artist Salvador Dali came sweeping through the dining room, cape and all! It was very unusual for a public person to attend Esalen and be so open about it. Many public people went there hoping for a private experience and they were able to have it. There was much discretion and privacy. Salvador Dali was just the opposite. He wore flamboyant clothes, colorful capes and swished them around his shoulders whenever out and about. He loved the attention and won the hearts of many other participants and staff.

People were drawn to Esalen to find comfort, like-minded people, and stimulating thoughts and ideas. The premise was to explore yourself, your decisions, the community, and find a way to go forward by adding something meaningful to this world. It usually was about challenge, self-confrontation and setting your own intention of how you wanted to live. Needless to say, it was a great retreat and workshop center.

Esalen also had hot tubs built around the hot springs that the region is famous for. I was forewarned that the hot tub experience was co-ed and nude, which I told thought was okay with me. At that time, I was finding myself as a strong, independent woman who would make my own choices. Nevertheless, I packed my one-piece black bathing suit.

My first intimidation was that the other members of my group were all male psychiatrists. My second was the expectation the first night after group to go to the hot tubs. Putting on my black bathing suit, I headed out to the candlelit paths. When I joined the groups in the hot tubs, I became the center of attention because I was the only one in a bathing suit. The next night, I was determined to become part of the group and not stand out in a crowd. After hanging my bathrobe on the hook, I got into the tub—nude. The next thing I knew, I was lying on a massage table with everyone standing around making sure I was okay. Apparently, the stress coupled with the heat caused me to faint and I went underwater to the bottom of the pool. Fortunately, there were others around to save me from drowning, and eventually I did become accustomed to the nude hot tubs; in fact, I rather enjoyed them, and I returned for thirteen more experiences at Esalen.

My experience there was so positive, in fact, that I went home to start an encounter group, and I joined a sensitivity group, went back to college for many years, found an inner sense of confidence. I even made sure I always had a hot tub in my home. Esalen had a profound impact on my life to this day: I love Bohemian clothing, good and healthy food is important to me, and love and acceptance of all is an important value to me.

Esalen (and later the same experience in a different setting—Miraval) is a concept that lives inside me - not just a place to visit.

"Esalen helps one savor life on the edge, literally and figuratively. Clothing was optional, self-questioning and growth were guaranteed".
–Sharon Cruse

Food Fuels the Body and Soul

Everyone has memories of food that stay with them. Just the thought can make them salivate and crave it. One of my strongest and most positive memories is of homemade bread. In my family, bread and dough had many meanings. Coming home from school and smelling cinnamon or caramel rolls just coming out of the oven is still with me. Of course, it wasn't simply the food that was so captivating. It meant that my mom and two of her best friends were seated in the kitchen and drinking hot coffee and telling wild tales. I would hop up and sit on the kitchen cupboard—never mind that the rolls had just been rolled out on those same counters—and the smell of spice and caramel filled the kitchen. To be right there, when the masterpieces came out of the oven, was to know deep pleasure.

Being part of the grown-up conversation also made me feel special.

In my family, each day had its special routine. Monday was for laundry, Tuesday was ironing, Thursday was cleaning. Sunday afternoon was when Dad would spin his own butter, enough to last the whole week. This just added to the pleasure and made coming home right after school every Wednesday—baking day—a real treat.

When Dad made the butter, I stood next to him cooking elbow pasta. My Sunday treat to myself was making tuna macaroni salad, flavored with homemade dill pickles, little cubes of cheddar cheese, and one drained can of peas. Only homemade mayonnaise could whip that dish into a masterpiece that I hid in the back of the refrigerator so I could treat myself for the next six days until I made again on the next Sunday. That first bowl after preparing with the mayo melting a bit because of the heat of the cooked pasta was a bit of heaven itself. The refrigerator was already stocked for that week with pickled pigs feet, herring in sour cream, homemade butter, and whatever meat my father could trade at his feedstore . I felt we ate like royalty, and I was set for the week .

The main dish that I still can't live without right now is "sour gravy." It's a Belgian dish that is layered this way:

- Fresh spring green dandelions (or today, large leaf or green lettuce—cold)
- Cubed boiled potatoes (hot)
- Cut up hard boiled eggs (cold)
- A few chopped red onions or best if green onions— both white and green parts
- And then the "gravy." Gravy is made with chopped bacon, a hot, thin white sauce made with flour and water, flavored with vinegar of your choice (malt or red wine).

Whether the origins are pure Belgian, French, or whatever—it's a dish you will never forget and come to crave often. It feeds your soul, wakes up your senses, and is a treat that you can enjoy again and again. For me, taking the time every couple of months today pays off. Food is more than taste. It's an experience to remember. Top this dish off with a warm caramel roll. It doesn't get much better than that combination.

> **"My best hostess tip is to have good food (whether homemade, take out, or delivery), good friends, and the best possible music."**
> —Sharon Cruse

Furniture Stores and Undertakers

In my little town, the funeral home was also the furniture store. At the time, I didn't know the background story of why this was. My father died at only forty-six years old. I visited my father there and said my final good-bye as the visitation and the viewing was in the back room My father was the first death I had ever dealt with—up close and personal. Little did I know that I would lose my best girl-friend two weeks later.

In my first experiences with death, (as a child), the deceased was laid out in a coffin and in the bay window of the living room of the family home. I attended several home viewings as a child, usually with my grandma. It was such a family affair. There was food everywhere for the mourners and the visitors, people sang, they drank in the kitchen and told many stories about the departed and their memories of him or her. Death was not something separate and sterile; it seemed like such part of life.

The furniture store, by contrast, didn't have the same comfort and family feel. Worse yet, this was my father, someone I loved dearly, and I had a hard time realizing that he was really gone at such a young age.

What I learned about the custom was this. In the 1800's, cabinet makers were called upon to make coffins. They often sold other furniture as well. A whole industry developed around both needs. They were craftsman and undertakers. Furniture stores and coffins went together. For many years, furniture stores and funeral homes were linked and owned by craftsmen. Eventually, they each became such big industries that they separated.

Now we have immense furniture stores and a funeral home industry. Its wasn't that way in my childhood. Watching the transition from home celebrations to today's memorials , one thing hasn't changed. People will die, their loved ones will gather and celebrate the deceased's life in whatever way speaks to that love. Often today, there are still prayers, food, gatherings, and a respect for the person who has died. Death, when it happens to someone you know and love, becomes a part of life.

"The fear of death follows from the fear of life. The person who lives fully is prepared to die at any time."
—Mark Twain

A Grand Night at the Grand Ole Opry

Sometimes, the stars line up for you just right if you just have a little patience.

I had no idea what to expect the first time I went to the Grand Ole Opry in Nashville, Tennessee. I only knew that I really liked the group the Oak Ridge Boys and that they sometimes played at the venue. I had been working twelve-hour days, seven days a week, and I needed a break. I felt like I needed to do something completely spontaneous and different, so I packed up my two teen girls and one foreign exchange student and decided to try and get last-minute tickets. This was before the Internet and cell phones, and when I called, I learned they were sold out, so we could try to come in case any seats opened up.

The girls were still game for a last-minute trip, though we had no idea how far Nashville was from Minneapolis, Minnesota. We arrived in Nashville just a few hours before showtime, went straight to the box office, but to no avail. We told our sad story and the workers looked sad and sorry, but nevertheless, it was almost showtime and there were still no tickets to be had. We accepted that fact, settled into our motel room, and planned to get a pizza for dinner and head back. We had left my name and the phone number of the motel with the box office in case anything changed.

While we were enjoying our pizza, the phone rang. We were in luck! We'd have to get there as soon as possible. Of course, we drove there practically on two wheels. Apparently, my name had been given to Randy Travis, the host for the night. When a performer is on stage and the audience has been seated, if there are any seats left over, the workers give the performer the list of people on waiting lists. The performer looks over the list, and if there is someone they would like to bring in, it is done. Unbeknownst to me, Randy Travis had read my book *Learning to Love Yourself* and recognized my name on the waiting list. Not only did we get into the show, but we were also treated to front row center seats.

The worker at the box office gave us the following message: "The agent recognized your name (said that one of your books saved someone in his family's life and they can always find four tickets)."

Minutes later, we were seated in our fantastic seats (all

complimentary) and enjoyed the Oakridge Boys, Randy Travis, Minnie Pearl, and countless other artists. We didn't know it, but it also just happened to be the night of the Country Music Awards, and there we were—right in the middle of it all. Needless to say, it was an amazing show, the best of the best! Our misfortune turned into something much better than we could ever have anticipated.

"I feel this is a family here, so kinda regardless of whatever happens in your life, you can always come home to the Grand Ole Opry."
—Ronnie Milsap

Hobos and Homeless

As a little girl, my life was greatly impacted by hobos. Today, we refer to people without a home as *homeless*. People often treat them as invisible, but they all have stories, and as a child their stories impacted me. Many became my friends, and I listened, learning a great deal from the sharing that took place. It was a rich time.

My grandma owned a beanery for the Great Northern Railroad. The trains would go through two little southern Minnesota towns, and often, two or three hobos would jump out of freight car and work their way into our town. If they hopped off the train, it meant they had enough coins to maybe search for food. This was the tail end of the Great Depression and these men (I never met a female hobo) needed food.

They had a language all their own. If a house was safe and willing to feed hobos, they would carve or draw a "safe sign" and put it on their house, which consisted of two circles with a line that went through both circles. Often, people would put out food—a pot of something, a loaf of bread, and, if it was the right season, freshly picked fruits or vegetables—near the sign and someone would come through and take them. I watched this process for a long time, and one day I asked my grandma if I could talk to them. She gave me instructions as to how to do that. Her rules were "never go farther than being able to see the house, be kind, and enjoy." I was careful and followed her instructions.

I would sit by the food and when someone saw the safe house sign on the door, they would come one at a time to take some food. My first question was always "Why are you a hobo?" The answers were all different. They were things like:

"My dad lost all his money, and we have no food at home . . ."

"My mom died, and we all had to leave our home and hopped on a train . . ."

"I have no home and the boxcar on the train is warmer than sleeping outside. Sometimes, I feel lonely, and the other riders are my friends . . ."

Some didn't want to talk; they took food and left as quickly as they came.

These were learning years for me. I was never afraid, and neither was my grandma. This was early 1940s. Sometimes, I would tell them I could walk to the end of the block, and we would, and then come back. In the meantime, if grandma was watching, she would put out some cookies for them. I was always fascinated, and every word they uttered spelled adventure to me.

Times changed by the time I was a mother in the 1960s. I felt the need to tell my children "Do not talk to strangers. Bad things could happen." What a loss that times have changed so much. When I see a homeless person, I still wonder what their story is all about, how they ended up in this situation.

"I'm not a vagrant . . . I'm a hobo. Big difference."
—Lee Child

Wrapped in the Generosity of Those Who Have Nothing

I had been hired to come to California to provide training for a corporation's employee assistance programs. The company offered a half-day workshop with me to local non-profit agency leaders. In that group was the Captain of the Los Angeles Salvation Army and the topic of workshop was "Facing and Dealing with Family Pain." After finishing my presentation, the Captain came to me and said, "I know a group of homeless women who live down around the Nickel, and they would so profit by hearing you speak—but they never will have that opportunity. Would you consider going to them?" What I knew of the Nickel in Los Angeles is that it is another name for skid row. "They are destitute, homeless, and forgotten by the mainstream. If this company is hiring you to establish an employee assistance program, perhaps you could volunteer a little time and speak to these women. I will provide your transportation."

I took that invitation to the corporation, and they agreed that on my future trips to LA, they would add one more night to my expense account and the Salvation Army would provide my transportation. That's how my workshop and lectures were delivered to about twenty women who would bring their grocery carts to gather under the one tree in the area, and my work with homeless women began. This went on for the length of time of my year-long contract. I went to Los Angeles about once a month, which was plenty of time to get to know the Salvation Army.

The women listened, they laughed, they got to know each other, and they gratefully remembered the families they came from and some that they had created and had not seen for years. Healing took place.

When my contract came to an end, it was sad for all of us. One woman came forward and handed me a sack. I was humbled that they had done this for me, and I was astonished to find the most beautiful off-white, pearl lace-like afghan that had been crocheted for me by these women. All their earthly goods were in the grocery carts they pushed, but somehow, they had purchased yarn, knitting needles, and worked on this piece of art, made with love.

That was many years ago and, to this day, when I am lonely, sad, or just not feeling well, I can wrap myself in love and honor and remember the "homeless women" in LA. It washes like a towel and gets better and more beautiful each time I use it.

"People who are homeless are not social inadequates. They are people without homes."
—Sheila McKechnie

Kotzebue, Alaska, Tang, and Bush Pilots

Alaska has many rules, regulations, and chatter about the use of alcohol. Years ago, I was part of a team of counselors, businesspeople, and various helping professionals working together to deliver a project bringing awareness of drug and alcohol addiction, among other things, to the community of Kotzebue in the Northwest Artic.

Some parts of Alaska were "dry," some were "damp." There were different rules and regulations from one area to the next, and some were seriously involved with the use of alcohol, which ranged from public drunkenness to poverty, abuse, illness, etc. My team was hired to come to Kotzebue and do what we could to provide education, jobs, structure, and improved family life to the people of the area, including the indigenous culture.

Change started by intervening in the primary structure of the town. We took several public officials, including the mayor, the superintendent of schools, some political leaders and several others, and brought them back to Minnesota with us where we had them enter into our in-patient treatment programs. Returning sober to their homes and community made a big impression on the townspeople and many locals were willing to give up the liquor that was regularly dropped off by bush pilots. A second benefit when the bush planes reduced their alcohol drop-offs was that there was also a lessening in dropping off jars of Tang (a powdered, artificially flavored orange drink) that was rotting the teeth of children. Mothers often used Tang instead of breastmilk for convenience much to the detriment of their children's health.

Over the years, some changes took hold, others were forgotten, and culture changed a little. However, my experience remains rich in my memory, and I have never forgotten my personal relationship with Kotzebue, Alaska, Tang, and meeting some of the bush pilots. It takes many people, various cultures, and interesting customs to make a world.

"True life is lived when tiny changes occur."
—Leo Tolstoy

**"I've always liked quiet people.
You never know if they are dancing in a dream or
if they're carrying the weight of the world."**
—John Green

Standing Up for Your Values:
Frank and the Minnesota 8

It was rare to find young men dodging the draft during World War II and the Korean conflict, but draft-dodging hit an all-time high when the United States got involved in Vietnam. The television news and daily newspapers showed graphic photos and videos, and young people protested the war on campuses from coast to coast. The country was divided, and it was an unsettling and conflicted time.

Vietnam was very different at its core from World War II and the Korean conflict, without a definite common enemy around which people could rally and justify sending their young to fight in a distant land. Baby Boomers came of age and there were many more young men in college at the time. It's been estimated that over 500,000 young men were involved in draft resistance.

My friend Frank was one of those men. He was a serious young man and fully believed that war and the draft were wrong. He was committed to high-quality peaceful education and also to peaceful protest. He stood behind his feelings and became part of the Minnesota 8 who raided a building and burned a significant numbers of draft cards (close to 10,000). He was arrested, convicted, and jailed in northern Minnesota for a few years.

I visited Frank when he was behind bars—my first experience of visiting someone in a federal prison, and the *clang* of the prison doors is a sound I will never forget. After Frank served his time and was released, he decided he wanted to become an elementary school teacher. The controversy about the war and the draft were stirred up again, but the town in which he wanted to work believed in Frank and hired him. He went on to teach about civic responsibility and peaceful protest for the rest of his career. He led me, and I'm sure all those who were his students, to think a great deal about values, choice, dedication and service. I still do. The Minnesota 8 helped shape many of my own ideas about war, draft, and the turbulent times that keep repeating themselves in our culture.

"Never waste your time trying to explain yourself to people who are committed to misunderstand you."
—Unknown

How It All Began: The National Association of Children of Alcoholics

So many people have been affected by alcoholism. When a child experiences this kind of pain, the impacts can last a lifetime and continue on to the next generation. We know this now, but this wasn't always understood.

Years ago, professional people were involved in the education or counseling for families facing some kind of addiction. They were from a wide range of backgrounds. Some were teachers, counselors, psychiatrists, public speakers, medical doctors, etc. They lived in different parts of the United States and each of these people were doing their own thing in their own communities. They were each known in their own circle but didn't have contact with others who were doing this work in other places.

Then came Joan Kroc. You may have heard her name. She was married to Ray Kroc, who founded the McDonald's hamburger chain. Joan lived in Santa Barbara, California, and she was very interested in the subject. She learned about the people who were doing this important work and contacted about six or seven of them, and it was suggested she bring them together and find a way to spread the message of hope and healing on a national level.

Joan sent each of them a first-class ticket and offered her ranch and staff for a weekend meeting to discuss this possibility. Little did she know each of them was an adult child who had come from an alcoholic family themselves. The group gathered at her ranch. I was one of those people. What Joan didn't anticipate was that we were all so touched to meet others who had been hurt by alcoholism in their families, that we spent the time experiencing relief and joy, but produced nothing for Joan to peruse—no suggestions. She was disappointed, but she understood. She invited each of us to go home and invite one more like-minded person and generously offered us a second ticket and four-day weekend at her ranch.

The rest is history. Our group met and before we left, we had formed the National Association of Children of Alcoholics. I was honored to be the first Chairman of the Board. That was in 1982, and since that time, thousands and thousands of adult children—those who grew up in a home where alcohol or other substances or behaviors were used—have been given hope, help, and experienced healing in their lives. Today, over forty years later, the work continues.

"Being the oldest child of an alcoholic parent is like being the only person awake in the back seat of a car while the rest of the occupants sleep peacefully—the car careens out of control and flies off the side of a cliff."
—Mary Kate DeCraene

No Toilet Paper? No Problem!

In 2020, at the start of the COVID-19 pandemic, store shelves were empty of many staples, including toilet paper, as people panic-shopped. I was concerned, but not in a frenzy. After all, no commercial toilet paper was a part of my very early experience. In our small community, when I was growing up, we did not have running water, nor did we have a septic tank or a way to dispose of today's version of toilet paper. Instead, we had chamber pots to use in a pinch in the middle of the night and outhouses. Our outhouse was about forty feet from the back door.

On long dark winter nights, the fairly short trip to the outhouse felt more like a mile. Therefore, we used the chamber pots which we could empty in the daylight. Our outhouse was a nice two-seater (for mothers and children) and had a half moon carved into the door. The carving was big enough for ventilation but not so big that critters would climb in for protection from the elements. Shoveling the walk in front of the house always included the very important path to the outhouse!

Rather than toilet paper, we were supplied with pages from the quarterly catalogs of Sears Roebuck and Montgomery Ward's. It wasn't the most comfortable way of finishing the trip to the bathroom, but it worked and was plentiful (there were four large catalogs a year).

Paper products were not used the way they are today. We didn't have facial tissues. We used handkerchiefs (a small square of beautiful fabric), which we put in the wash every day. Women's handkerchiefs were floral, had pastel colors, and hopefully matched each outfit. Farmers had big, red squares. Businessmen sported white handkerchiefs that they put in the front of a suit pocket. There was no such thing as disposable diapers. In those days, diapers were cloth, and the used ones were dropped in a diaper pail half filled with water and bleach, and hopefully washed every three or four days. These were very different times but are clear in my mind today.

With today's many brands of soft, strong, quilted, medicinal, colorful and patterned toilet papers, multiple brands of facial tissues, and disposable diapers, you can begin to see why I didn't panic with the idea of the 2020 toilet paper shortage. There is always a way!

**"The best seat in the house. Please remain
seated for the entire performance."**
—Anonymous

The Art and Artistry of
Salvador Dali and Bill Rainey

I have been fortunate to have been inspired and touched by art and artists. When I was younger, my husband Joe and I traveled often. We visited museums every chance we could. My style was to visit each floor, taking in as much possible. Joe, on the other hand, could usually be found far behind me on the first floor, reading all the details about the art and the artist. We truly appreciated how art personally spoke to us.

My life was touched by meeting two great artists. The first was Salvador Dali. Imagine my surprise when the door opened at the Esalen Institute and this man who looked just like Salvador Dali came into the room. He had a signature mustache, wore a cape, and had an air of mystery and flourish. When he introduced himself, I discovered that he didn't just look like Salvador Dali, he was Salvador Dali. Although I always admired his paintings, getting to know him as a person made me like him even more, and he was one of the people who taught me that the artist is as interesting and his or her work.

I was ready for a relaxing Sunday afternoon when I took a call from Bill Rainey. I didn't answer my own calls at that time. My secretary at work and my answering machine at home filtered all my calls.

On that particular day, however, I was looking for something in my office. When I answered, Bill Rainey said, "Good morning, my name is Bill Rainey."

"Good morning, my name is Sharon," I answered. That call became the start of a relationship that I treasure to this day. Not only did I get to know Bill Rainey "the artist" but also his wife Ann. Ann has graced me with her talent and work and Bill simply moved into my heart with his beliefs and artistry (and the dapper way he dresses). He also taught me two important lessons: A master seeks perfection; an artist seeks expression; and a deep appreciation of Impressionism.

Bill and Joe were soul buddies and brothers. They trudged destiny's road together and Ann and I remain great friends. Bill graced me with a beautiful painting several years ago and it is entitled "Another Chance." It remains one of my greatest treasures. I feel inspired by both great artists.

"A true artist is one who inspires others . . ."
—Salvador Dali

Getting to Know the US Secret Service—Up Close and Personal

During the years of Joe's and my friendship with President Ford and Betty Ford, a major experience was learning how to be around the Secret Service. It was unique, to say the least. They were always present and nearby, but you barely knew they were there. We just got used to their presence, which made us feel safe and protected, but on the other hand made us feel cautious, like, *why is this constant companionship needed?* Most often, I had a sense of awe. How it all works is a masterpiece of coordination. We boarded airplanes, ate lunch, and watched performances—just like everyone else around us. Yet there was the presence of guarding, watching, and alertness that filtered in, making our small group different. The Secret Service was always in the front seat with the driver, Joe and Betty, the two speakers, were in the middle, and I sat with President Ford and in the back. We often joked about being in the background.

Three memories in particular stand out for me. One was when Joe and I were having lunch in Beaver Creek with Betty and Jerry. We were served dessert, which was topped with red, plump, strawberries. Betty took one and said to the agent, whose name I don't recall, ". . . Here, I know you love these." She handed a big, juicy strawberry to an agent who all of a sudden appeared beside her. To this day, I don't know where he came from. He just showed up at her side!

Another time, when I first started getting to know Betty Ford, we were driving to a furniture design center. The car stopped, and my automatic response was to reach for the handle to open the door. Out of nowhere, a hand was on top of my hand, accompanied by kind but strong words, "Never touch a door handle." I learned very quickly to wait for someone to open the door for me.

My third, favorite memory was when a friend of Betty asked me if I would teach her how to make a public presentation. We went to the bedroom, and I started to move a piece of furniture around to set up a mock podium. Betty and her friend were talking about clothes, and then President Ford came in looking for the sock he dropped on the floor. He had just discovered he had put on two different colored socks. I looked up and the Secret Service agent, standing stoically as always, gave me a wink at all the activity. I felt like I was in an Andy Warhol painting that was a bit surreal!

**"To become an agent, the individual must be trained,
a US citizen, between ages of 21 to 37. Have a bachelor's
degree and three years of work service in criminal
investigation or law enforcement. Vision needs to be 2020
correctable, take a drug test, and pass a polygraph.**
—Ronald Kessler

Soup-Can Communication

In this day of instant communication and social media, its hard for most people to imagine what life was like when I was growing up in my hometown of Comfrey, Minnesota. I really liked the young people across the way, but winter snowstorms often meant going days without seeing my best friend. We could usually meet up at school but talking on the phone back then was difficult.

We had party lines, where anyone could listen in to your conversation, which didn't offer much privacy. Our phone number was 37218 and our business was 37217. Home was two shorts and a long (ring). The business was one long and two shorts. That's how we knew the call was for us and pick up the phone. There were also four other families on the same line and they each had their own ring. Usually, we let the system work. However, if interested or bored, we could carefully pick up the phone, hold our hand over the mouthpiece, and listen in on the party line and hear others' conversations. It also meant they could listen in to ours as well.

If we wanted our own private conversation, we had to take matters into our own hands. We went the low-tech way: a tomato soup can phone. As soon as it was warm enough to open the windows in my bedroom in the spring and summer, which also filled my room with the fragrance of blooming lilacs, we would set up soup can communication. We strung heavy cord between my bedroom window and the window down the street. We could then write private and secret messages, put them in the soup can, tie the can to the cord and pull it back and forth to communicate. We could share so much juicy gossip and private plans with no fear of being intercepted.

To this day, I only use the phone for important business and often private business. The idea of using technical communication to meet social needs does not appeal to me. My preference is to communicate and meet in person whenever possible. I like eye-to-eye connection.

As for canned soup, I eat very little except for Campbell's tomato, on the side with a grilled cheese sandwich.

"Styles come and go, design goes on forever, solving communication problems with new tools applied to the same old common sense."
—Ivan Chermayeff

From Trash to Treasure

Living in Jasper, Minnesota, there was only a five-and-dime variety store, a grocery store, a gas station and stores that catered to a small rock quarrying community. There were no museums, shopping centers, big box stores, artifacts stores, workshops, or libraries.

It was slim pickings for a curious child. However, about a mile out of town, was the dump, where people threw their trash. It was not the kind of garbage one would see in a landfill today. All inedible food was fed to animals or composted. The dump had discarded items like old boxes, containers, jewelry, and blankets, among other things They were thrown in a pile and each season big tractors came and ground it up. Then people would start all over again bringing their unwanted items.

Believe it or not, this place was a delight for me and my friend Janice. We would take our big bags and look for treasures. It might be an old book, an empty storage box, sometimes what looked like jewelry, a statue, old decorating items, small items of furniture, plants, dishes, and on and on. We took our finds home each trip, washed them up, and found things to do with these special things we found. I started a small library in the corner of my room. I decorated for a season, sometimes throwing my finds away and discovering new and even more updated valuable treasures. The search was part of the fun and the learning.

It was only much later when I went to school and could read about some of my treasures did I realize the gift I had received on lazy days when Janice I would comb through countless items, looking for the one that deserved going home with us and could continue to broaden our curiosity. I grew to appreciate these items, and it set a spark in me for the later-in-life experiences, when I could visit museums, libraries and enjoy artifacts from around the world. This appreciation of all items that carry history and tell the story of the people who owned tangible treasures in their hands was birthed in me when I was seven, eight, and nine years old. I was a lucky child. Many years later, I still have a few of those treasures. As they say, "One person's junk is another person's treasure."

"There is no such thing as "away."
When we throw anything away,
it must go somewhere."
–Annie Leonard

Small-Town Living

Even if you never lived in a small town, chances are you've visited one or knew someone who grew up in one. "Small town" to me meant 547 people on most days. Now that's small! But it was the perfect size for growing up.

My hometown was proud of our Catholic grade school (eight grades) and our public grade school (also eight grades). We shared a high school. We had seven different Lutheran churches and one big Catholic church. Main street sported a Red Owl grocery store, a meat market with fresh meat (butchered from local farms), my dad's chicken hatchery and livestock feed store, a men's clothing store (Axels) and a store for ladies called The Fashion Shop. (The women's fashion shop sold items that only women used, and those items were sent home in brown paper bags.) They tried to be discreet, but you really didn't want to be noticed carrying a little brown bag. There were three gas stations, a town hall, (which converted to a roller rink on weekends}, a hardware store, a dry cleaner, a telephone operator office, a small hospital (eight beds). a doctor's office, a post office, one cafe, one liquor store, and a very active beer parlor and pool hall. We enjoyed a move theater with weeknight evening shows and a matinee on Sunday afternoons. Snyder's drug store sported a soda fountain and ice cream. We also had a grain elevator. a depot, and train stop. A block from Main Street, there was a lumber yard and factory. The town supported the main town and a suburb called Liberty Park (population forty-two people) and multiple farms until you ran into the other small towns: Darfur, Springfield, and St. James. Just outside town was the cemetery. Everyone of all faiths or no faith ended up there.

Life in a small town meant everyone knew everyone else and supported one another. You also didn't have secrets. It felt secure in our town, one belonged and your family wasn't limited to blood relatives. In my growing up years, I was in most homes and my friends all loved my home. They were welcome there. To this day, it's my belief that my career came from my high school business teacher and my speech coach. My education was twofold: "structured" with twelve years of school and "personal experience" of the style of small-town living. It was a time of innocence, maybe the last of its time. I appreciate being part of the mystique.

"The bad thing about living in a small town was that everything became a personal issue. The good thing about living in a small town was that everything became a personal issue. During times of trouble, support system was massive."
–Linda Howard

Underground Las Vegas

Most people go to Las Vegas for the gambling. Joe and I never gambled there, but we took in all the major shows and many of the lounge shows—there's nothing better than the Rat Pack at The Sands. Occasionally, you could catch two or three informally showing up and singing songs, but all their famous shows as a group were at The Sands. I am talking Frank Sinatra, Sammy Davis, Jr., Dean Martin and, in our day, Peter Lawford. Joe and Peter had a professional connection. We saw some informal times. Right place, right time. Las Vegas happenings were the norm.

One night, a recognized singer came on stage at the MGM. He was followed by another recognized and very famous singer. One made a comment about the other's wife and singer #1 walked over, grabbed the hand of singer #2, and broke his thumb. We saw it happen and, of course, all the details were in the *Las Vegas Review* the next day. The audience was aghast and gasped. I held my breath. Security came out, removed the singers and the next thing we knew, out walked Bob Hope and turned into a comedy sketch. Joe knew Bob Hope fairly well, so all this activity had interest to us. Sometimes, in a Las Vegas show, reality is the show!

We were exhausted and emotionally wrung and just didn't want to face the crowds leaving the theater, so just this once, we tried to take a shortcut out a door that said, "Do Not Enter." Instead of ending up in the parking lot, we found ourselves in the old amusement park that was closed behind the MGM. It was dark and scary. The rides and the side shows were dark and simply abandoned. We inched along a fence and then had to go down into the underground tunnels. We saw the city that lives underground, and it was a sight. It was about a three-block area before we could see light and way out.

Finally, we followed the path to the light and came up out of the tunnels in a different casino and worked our way back through that casino to the streets. Between the skirmish on stage and the life in the tunnels, we saw a part of Las Vegas few get to see—and something that is never advertised.

Many would find it hard to believe, but I saw it with my own eyes!

"I have visited many places over the course of my life— both near and exotic. Underground life under the city of Las Vegas ranks right up there with one of the most interesting experiences!
—Sharon Cruse

Chapter Three
Family Connections

Did You Love Your Dad?

Ask any person if they loved their dad, and you will get as many answers as you ask people. Some dads were great, some not so much. Some bland and boring while some were bullies and dangerous. Some made many bad decisions that made the whole family suffer.

I loved my dad most of the time, though not always. Later on, because of his alcoholism, it got harder for me. One of the many early reasons I loved him was the way he treated my high school girlfriends. His business was on the way home from my grade school and high school and my friends would stop in and say hello as we walked home. He was always so friendly and usually gave us money to put in the cola machine so we could have a soda on the way home.

It didn't matter if I had one friend with me or several. He always had enough coins.

I also loved my dad for spinning homemade butter every Sunday morning and for teaching me the polite habit of being on time. He gave me rewards for being early or on time, which helped me to learn the importance of this lesson. He used to say, "if you are on time, you are ten minutes late." My dad always gave rewards. It could be a pastry in the morning for me and my friends or an extra quarter. Even with his expectations (be early), I always felt resected and appreciated.

One of his tenderest moments was when I was going to attend my high school senior prom. My date was Kenny Ryan. My dress had beautiful red roses with an overlay jacket with faded red roses. It was spectacular. I was the only one of my close group of four girls to have a date. About a week before prom, when our excitement was peaking, my dad enlisted my mom's help and sent out date invitations to my three girlfriends. He asked them all out to dinner on prom night in a nearby town at a new restaurant that was considered "special." On prom night, my date Kenny picked me up and dad left our house with three corsages for my girlfriends. He drove my mom and friends out for a very special dinner in the nearby town. I really loved my dad that night.

Sometimes, my dad showed me how he loved me (spinning butter on Sunday mornings, driving me to school in the rain or snow, teaching me to drive, etc.). Sometimes my dad would "teach" me something rather than just talk about it. I loved him so.

"You were braver than you believe, stronger than you think and more loved than you knew."
—Winnie the Pooh

Driving in the Ditches

The small town in which I grew up was surrounded by land divided up in squares. Each square was called a section and each section was one square mile. A walk around the section was four miles. There were local roads that had no names, and a few bigger roads that did have names—Elm Street, Main Street, Liberty Street—you get the picture. All roads near my hometown fell into this pattern. If you strung sections together, there was usually one path/road that became the primary road that actually went to somewhere other than a farm. One road out of town led to Darfur, a small town with only two bars and a general store. Another led to Springfield, a bigger community with almost three small blocks of retail stores. The third way out of town led to Butterfield, which had a meat packing building, and the fourth way out of town led to Mountain Lake, another town about the same size as my hometown. Some roads were surrounded by crops, and some had ditches.

As a child, it was interesting to me to try to figure out why my dad preferred to drive in ditches rather than on the main road. It puzzled me why he only drove home from Darfur in the ditches. In Darfur, my dad would visit with the other businessmen and share some beers, and I would swing on the swing set outside or play in the playground with all the children. On other occasions, he would drive home on the main road. As a little girl, I tried to figure out this pattern. He was my father, and I was a little girl, so I didn't think to ask. As time went on, and the weeks went by, he found a way to make the ride between Darfur and Comfrey even more exciting. He would leave Darfur and drive into the open fields. Picture a field full of plowed rows of soil. The plow left ridges that were about eight inches high. Instead of driving "with" the ridges, he drove across them and gave us a bumpy ride as we scaled the top of the ridges. We bumped along and it was fun. It was almost like a carnival ride as we bounced in our seats. I thought it was really a clever idea.

Finally, I grew older, and my curiosity got the best of me, and I just needed to ask. He replied ,"Young lady, it's my choice to drive in the ditches. It's much safer that way." He went on to explain, "You know that after I have a few beers, my driving isn't as good, and I never want to take a chance on the main road. In the ditch, I can't possibly run into another car, and so it's the safer way to drive home. It's for your protection and for mine." It all made sense to me.

I pursued my questioning. "Why do you drive across the bumpy fields, Daddy?"

He said, "That was just for fun!"

It all made sense to me. Perhaps it would be good to not have those beers, but at least he made the best decision to be safe.

"THINK! The safe way is the best way"
—Catherine Mayhe

Another Chance at Family Roles

In 1976, I had no extra money to follow dreams, but I took a chance anyway. My dream was finding a way to share all that I had experienced as a child, and all I was learning as a family therapist, with many other families who might be having similar struggles with dysfunctional family systems. It was clear to me that there were behavioral patterns in a family, that they were fluid, and that they were repeated in many system dynamics. Over and over, I saw and experienced the same patterns. Once addressed and behavior changes were made, both the individual and the family system became healthier. At that time, I was working at an alcohol intervention center. I wrote up my ideas about those patterns and how to address them and wrote a small booklet describing my thoughts. I gathered what little money I could spare and printed fifty copies of the booklet and distributed them as handouts in a class I was teaching in a university about human behavior. People snapped them up, and I had requests for more.

They were expensive to print, so I started charging a dollar a copy to help cover my costs. The company I worked for, however, claimed the booklet was their original work.

Not being experienced in business at that time, I nevertheless instinctively knew that this booklet was important, and I was glad that I had copyrighted it the year before as my material.

The yearlong distribution in the class I taught was a key factor in securing the copyright at that time. The roles I created, that of Family Hero, Scapegoat, Lost Child, and Mascot, were mine and officially copyrighted in 1976. Those roles played a key part in my first book, which became a bestseller, entitled *Another Chance: Hope and Health for the Alcoholic Family*.

Imagine my thrill of walking into counseling centers in Australia, Germany, and England and seeing those roles on posters hanging in counseling and medical offices. The book was translated into other languages and has been distributed around the world.

Oftentimes, life unfolds by chance rather than by any plans we make.

"Take risks. Ask big questions.
Do big things, make mistakes, and start again.
Take charge of your own destiny."
—Sharon Cruse

Grandma's Love Is Special

I remember the smells first. They were always there when grandma was there.

There were the smells of great food. Hamburgers and onions, fried chicken, and of course, her signature dish: homemade donuts. Long before donut shops, my grandma had about twenty kinds of donuts she would make whenever she came to visit or in the cafe where she worked in as a cook. Her specialty was cinnamon sugar or pumpkin spice. If I close my eyes, I can still imagine the smell and the taste of them.

There were the scents of my grandma herself, her Blue Waltz perfume and face powder. When she was done working and it was "grandma's time," on would go the perfume and face powder, and she was ready to play the piano (by ear, not by note). I loved to hear her version of the popular songs of the time.

We were poor, but I didn't know it. She always had a way of making me feel special. We used to ride on the Great Northern Railway. She would get free tickets to ride the train because she worked in a beanery (cafe) and the conductors loved her food. She would always bring a basket with homemade sandwiches and cookies and tell me. "We are so lucky to have homemade food. We don't have to go to the dining car and eat at a table. You are special." I grew up believing that we were the lucky ones and didn't find out we were poor until much later.

Grandma was kind. I still have my grandma's bank book and saw she never had more than $350.00 in the bank at any one time. The dates in her book are from 1946. With that income, she was able to raise four children who lived until old age, adopt a brother and sister whose parents were killed in an accident, the Ihoos family, and raised them to adulthood. She cared for a husband who was disabled and became the family breadwinner.

She loved all her grandchildren and earned her role as "favorite gramma" and as the most accepting person I ever met. She planned her own funeral, which was exceptional, and she gave all of us our kindness role model.

She danced, she traveled on the Greyhound Bus Line and introduced all of us to the Great Northern Railway and travel.

If I close my eyes, I can still remember her, surrounded by love.

**"We need more than information in
our lives, we need wisdom."**
—Anderson Cooper.

"May her life be an enduring message."
—Sharon Cruse

Saying Farewell to Grandma:
A Life of Amazing Grace

In planning for my husband's service, a "celebration of his life," I went back to a memory of my beloved Grandma Olson's funeral and the impact it had on me. At her death, I was the oldest of nineteen grandchildren. My grandma was one of the major impactful people in my childhood. She believed that "while it would be good if her children loved her when she died, it would be more important to her as a mother that they loved each other." She usually followed her talk with her actions, and she set about to make that happen. In my

case, there was a rift between me and my uncle about whether or
not I should be able (as a divorced woman) receive communion in
the Catholic church. I said yes, he said no, and we didn't talk about
it. He was quite firm. The family all knew of the rift. All of a sudden,
during her funeral service, at the time of going to the front in this
small-town Catholic church, he walked over to me and held out his
hand to assist me to the communion railing to receive communion. I
was shocked and took his hand and went to communion for the first
time in a long time.

Later I would find out that Grandma Olson, in my behalf called
him to her deathbed and made my reconciliation with church one
of her last wishes. He listened, then agreed and made the first offer.
While today, it wouldn't matter to me to have his invitation, at that
time of my life, it was most healing and powerful. Grandma was
always working behind the scenes.

Her funeral was a true celebration that she planned just the way
she envisioned it—a testament to her loving belief system, her faith,
and her love of family. She wanted a white blanket placed across the
casket for her pure initiation into the heavens and she wanted her
grandchildren to walk her into the church and follow her casket. As
the oldest, I went first and my eighteen first cousins followed me.
She requested that all the ladies wear Easter hats (even though it
was nowhere near Easter), and she wanted the processional to be
"The Easter Parade." Everyone had a story about grandma. As the
ceremony progressed, she had requested that each child and grandchild bring a gift for her to take on her journey and that they put
these gifts in the casket with her. I remember taking a bottle of Mogen
David sweet wine. She always had a tiny glass before she went to bed
at night, and I wanted her to continue her customs. We closed the

celebration with the song with "Amazing Grace." If anyone ever had amazing grace, it was my Grandma Olson.

**"To all grandmas—your lives have been full of loving deeds,
forever thoughtful—today and tomorrow,
you will be cherished."**
—Sharon Cruse

Grandpa's Wisdom

It's easy to teach a grandson skills, like how to fly a kite, throw a ball, cook a meal, or drive a car. Imparting values to last a lifetime are harder. One grandson, Matthew, is now thirty-one, and he tells a meaningful story about his grandpa. He told me that Grandpa always shared his truth. One day, when Matthew was about twelve or thirteen, Grandpa told him the story of his addiction to alcohol and how tough it was treating that addiction and making lifestyle changes. At this point, Grandpa had about forty-seven years of sobriety. Matthew reported that this honest sharing made him uneasy because he had learned that addiction was a bad thing. And he never thought of Grandpa as "bad." He found the whole discussion rather uncomfortable, but never forgot the lesson he learned that day. When he was grown up, he realized that his grandpa shared a slice of life that brought around great intimacy and deep sharing.

When Matthew was about fifteen, Grandpa had another moment of sharing that made him uneasy. Whenever they parted, Grandpa always said, "I love you." He did it easy and that was his familiar way of saying good-bye. One day, Grandpa simply said, "You never tell me that you love me. You just say good-bye." Not being in an age of touchy-feely communication, this conversation stood out. Once again, there was a lesson in this exchange. That deep sharing caused some deep thinking and, one day, when Matthew was leaving, he looked at Grandpa and said, "Love ya." It felt awkward the first time but much easier as time went by. He said that the exchange felt good and whenever the two ended a visit, they both said "Love ya" at the end. That included Matthew's last visit with Grandpa, just before he died.

"Every generation revolts against its fathers and makes friends with its grandfathers."
—Lewis Mumford

"More and more, when I single out the person who inspired me most, I go back to my grandfather."
—James Earl Jones

Learning to Drink Alcohol

As a young girl, I witnessed many drinking parties in my home. They were usually on Saturday nights and Sunday afternoons, and it appeared that everyone was having fun, sharing stories and laughing. Aunts, uncles, parents, and friends all gathered to "have a few drinks." At my house, we celebrated everything: starting a new job, quitting a job; first communions and confirmations; summer is coming, fall is coming, winter is coming; fishing and hunting; trips, birthdays, anniversaries, weddings . . . and the list could go on forever. There was drinking every week, with obviously very few consequences. People had a drink, shared each other's company, and socialized.

My father, who wanted to teach me everything (bookkeeping, gardening, making homemade butter, how to do business, how to count baby chickens five at a time, how to drive a car, etc.) decided it was time for me to learn to drink alcohol. I was twelve years old. It was different times, a different era, and different knowledge. At that time, there were flavored vodkas (orange, lemon, lime, cherry, etc.) He mixed some lime vodka and a bit of fizzy soda of some kind.

After a few cubes of ice, I tried it and really felt it was no big deal. On Sundays, when the parties were going on, he would make me a small cocktail. That was part of my growing-up years. I really thought it was enjoyable at the time and drinking a bit of alcohol on Sunday afternoons continued to be no big deal. Addiction is a serious disease, and either one is addicted to the mood-altering substance, or they are not. Fortunately, I was not dependent on a mood change, while someone else could have had the same experiences and be an alcoholic today.

Later, because I was a serious child and teen, I never tried beer, wine, or anything except my father's cocktail at family parties. In high school, I didn't know anyone in my small-town school who drank alcohol, including beer—the entire time I was in high school. I stopped going to family parties many Sundays and started spending more time with my friends. That ended my experiences with alcohol.

Once I graduated from high school, I grew up, and went off on my own. I married early, and I married someone who didn't drink at all. Alcohol wasn't part of my life. Soon, I was pregnant, so I would never have endangered myself or my child. I didn't think about alcohol again until I was about thirty-three, when, at a dinner party, a friend offered me a glass of white wine. Another time, someone offered me a mixed drink and I enjoyed it as well.

To this day, I enjoy a good glass of wine or a gin and tonic. However, alcohol remains no big deal.

"Alcoholism is a fatal disease. It's a killer disease and we live in a society that nurtures it. We must become aware of the difference between an abstainer, an alcohol user, an alcohol abuser and an alcoholic who has a disease."
—Sharon Cruse

"Some drink alcohol as a beverage and some are dependent on alcohol."
—Vern Johnson

A Mother's Love

It's been said that "giving birth to a child is like having your heart walk around outside your body." To me, my gray-haired children are still "the kids," and when your child cries, you cry. When they celebrate, you smile. The more children, the more pieces of you walking around. One is never quite the same after having given birth.

I was quite young when my children were born, so we grew up together. It was like a child having a child. I grew a bit with each facet of their growth. By the time my youngest was fully grown, so was I. Together, we learned to care, to trust, to let go, to lead, to support, to step aside and, so very important—how to take responsibility, how to have fun, how to belong, and how to love.

Motherhood is demanding. It's 24/7 and changes everything. My mom was mother, wife, employee, sister, aunt, and friend. I watched and I felt. It was good for me to have a working mom. It was a great lesson for me. At times, my life needed me to be full-time mom; at other times, a student; at other times an employee; and eventually an employer. Learning the dance of roles and responsibilities taught me many lessons. I had already learned many of the lessons by watching my grandmother. She was a powerhouse. Lessons learned from my mom and grandma as a child made me a better mother. They were "whole" women and took on each of their roles with passion and hard work.

It is my hope that as I watch my girls also mother, that they know all of their potential and responsibility. The success of their children (my grandchildren) tells me every day that the mothering gene runs through another generation.

I say this but also want to say that we should not forget the fathers. One of my sources of great pride and pleasure is watching my grandson parent his daughter. It does seem as though the link between generations is love and wisdom.

"Motherhood is messy and hard.
And challenging, and crazy, and sleepless,
and giving and still unbelievably beautiful."
—Rachel Martin

My Sister Sue: A Beautiful Flower Gone Too Soon

My younger sister, Sue, was one of a kind. Perhaps that was no clearer than the day when my family had a small family reunion within a major family reunion. When all the relatives came together, there were eighty-seven of us. We were all descended from four sisters: Stella, Irene, Edith, and Mary. We all are part of the Rae Clan of Scotland. I am a descendent of Mary Rae (my grandma Olson). At the reunion, each descendent of each of the four matriarchs wore a different color shirt to the party to distinguish whose lineage you were a part of. Our family's color was red. I went so far as to provide all the red T-shirts with name, date of the party, and other information printed on them. We were all so happy to belong to this tribe, that is, except for my sister. Sue didn't like the color red, so she showed up in a flowered one-piece pantsuit. She looked like a doll, but she clearly didn't want to be part of the clan. Sue was always purposefully different and stood out in a crowd.

This was the way she chose to live her life. As the youngest in our family of three children, she missed out on a great deal of the joy and connection that was such a big part of my life. I knew our family when it was happy, full of hope and joy; young, healthy, and so connected. I was alone as a happy and favored first child and first grandchild and was doted upon by my grandma and all the aunts and uncles. Then the alcohol increased—my father was the first drinker, later my mother abused prescription medication and also became an alcoholic—the hatchery burned down, money became scarce again, and my parents lost their dreams. She and I grew up in two separate families.

My brother was born five years after me and Sue five years after that. They grew up when dreams were shattered and tension was high. We knew our families very differently.

Sue craved beauty, inner peace, comfort, control, and the life force. She created amazing gardens (so massive and beautiful that people had weddings there). She grew much of her own food, canned and preserved good food, she dressed stylishly, she wore only Erno Lazio makeup. She loved perfumes and we could spend a whole long distance phone call comparing fragrances. Another call just might be about toffee recipes. She brought light, fun, fashion, and the love of beauty into our family. The family loved Sue and Sue loved the family. When someone in a family is a bit eccentric, love continues. I have always wondered if her quest for beauty, appreciation of the fine things in life, her love of all animals—especially dogs—and her unquenchable thirst to grow beautiful flowers and healthy vegetables had anything to do with the deprivation that our parents' drinking and smoking had on her young life.

I will always be grateful for all the joy Sue brought into my life, and I was lost and devastated by her shocking diagnosis of cancer and her death from it only a couple of months later. Her special place and light in my life was dimmed way too soon. Younger sisters are not supposed to die quickly and disappear right out of my life. Shine on—you left a beautiful path for me to follow. I'll miss you always.

"Sisters are different flowers
from the same garden."
—Unknown

"I'd rather have flowers
than diamonds."
—Emma Goldman

"Hello, Son"

My father never used the word orphan. It was too painful. He was abandoned by his mom and his dad died shortly thereafter. He was seven years old when she left. As she ran away from her home, she had her two youngest boys in each hand. They didn't know they were leaving their abusive, alcoholic father. As she started to board the bus to take her to freedom, they both broke loose and ran as fast and far as they could. They were afraid if they left on the bus, their father would find them and hurt them. She looked back, boarded the bus, and my father did not see her for thirty years. He never heard a word from her. He and his brother went back home. His father continued his drinking and died within a year. At that point, the boys were taken in by the owner of a farm and they became farmhands in exchange for boarding. Life had started for my dad in a painful way.

As any child would, he wanted people to love and who loved him back. He worked hard toward that goal and reached much of it as a result of his love and his efforts to make it happen. He married and started his own family.

We were living in Comfrey, Minnesota, and on Dad's thirty-seventh birthday, he received a card. It was simply signed "Mother." As you can imagine, this was surprising and very emotional. He called everyone in his family of origin (seven siblings). He tried to find someone to go with him to find his mother. The only thing we had to go on was the return postmark of New Port Richey, Florida. Within the month, my dad packed my mom, me, my brother and sister, and his oldest sister in his car and we headed to Florida. There, we checked with post office boxes, neighbors, people on the street. We asked questions, we told stories, and finally someone said, "I know someone who talks about Minnesota a lot. Maybe she has lived there." He sent us to a restaurant. He asked to speak to the owners, and they came to introduce themselves. Preparing to tell his story all over again, he said, "Hello, my name is . . .

The woman waited a few minutes, and then said " Hello, Son."

That simple statement led to a two-year reunion when his mother came back to Minnesota and met all her children and grandchildren. She still had two siblings herself that were left in our little town. Everyone met her and loved her. Of course, there were questions and much sharing. As you can imagine, that day at the bus depot left her feeling horrible, scarred, and in pain. However, there was no anger, blame, or resentment.

Everyone relished those two years and shared information, hugs, and reconciliation. Then she simply died of a combination of old age and a stroke. It was a joy to know some of the stories, and to see my father so happy to finally meet and know his mom. She, too, was so happy to know him. They spent hours together and some piece of his life came together for him. It taught me pure acceptance as I watched these relationships unfold before my eyes. That lesson has provided strength, courage, and wisdom in many parts of my life. One never knows the indirect lessons that our parents teach us through the years. Life is often so much more interesting than fiction.

"Children without families are the most vulnerable people in the world."
—Brooke Randolph

Chapter Four
Humor

Boots Are Made for Walking

Boots are important to me. Some people collect shoes, I collect boots. Actually, only three styles of boots are what make my heart sing. My first pair came from an employer in Texas. They initiated me into the Austin, Texas, society scene, consisting of hats, gowns—and boots. I was a serious workshop speaker and trainer at that time, working out of Minnesota. She offered me a great deal of income (which would certainly help my family) and she said I could put her company on the map with my speaking skills. However, she said I needed to fit in with people who would donate money to a good cause and "Minnesota nice" wasn't going to help. She offered to assist me in fitting in with Austin, Texas, society.

Gift number one was a pair of navy-blue cowboy boots with turquoise lizard skin inserts. With my Texas hat adorned with pheasant feathers, I looked real Austin. It worked. The donors were there. I attended balls, charity events, and wore beautiful gowns, either purchased or rented. I had developed a type of "family of origin" intervention and treatment that worked. She built the treatment center in Austin in an old historic mansion, and I was the seller who closed the deals. Many families received some of the best treatment offered in this country. I wore those boots until they were unwearable and then joined the Texas custom of hanging old worn-out boots on fences. (She also gifted me with red down winter boots and that story will be told later in "The Red Rose.")

Perhaps my greatest influence on loving boots was from my son Pat. Looking over the boot options one winter, seeing Uggs advertised, they were clearly my taste and type. The price tag was a bit of shock. I let him know they were too expensive for my taste. My decision was to move on down the line, settling for Ugg lookalikes. That Christmas, however, Pat had a different idea and bought me my first pair of Uggs—the real thing. Eight years later, I have never looked back. My Uggs now come in different colors and make my heart sing, even finding a dry cleaner that keeps them looking tip top. Halloween means that Ugg wearing begins and one pair or another, they don't come off until after Easter. These boots are made for walking.

"Life is a party to which you've been invited.
Join in or sit on the sidelines."
—Sharon Cruse

" When life gives you rainy days, wear cute
and comfortable boots and jump in the puddles."
—adapted from Winnie the Pooh

Dress for Success

As a public speaker, I loved clothes, and I sought to find a new outfit for every major national event at which I presented. I remember being very excited to find a pair of reading glasses that had the same black polka dots on the frames as the dress I was wearing. The fact I can remember and connect the presentation with an outfit tells you how serious I took the presentation. Some of my presenting outfits included:

The black-and-white polka dot dress and matching glasses. One person in the audience confessed to me, "I didn't hear much of what you said, but seeing you lecture in that outfit gave me the message, 'I want what she has, and I am willing to work for it.'"

Often a bright red dress with gold jewelry. Red is bold and speakers need to be bold.

Sometimes, total black if it felt like a very serious subject.

Bright, almost psychedelic prints if it was to be a fun or wellness workshop. Lectures usually started with a smile.

Cowgirl Western if it was in the Black Hills of South Dakota, complete with pheasant-feathered denim hat.

Crisp suits if it was to present Grand Rounds at Harvard Medical School.

Leather and silver jewelry if the Sturgis, South Dakota, motorcycle rally was going on as it did every August.

Tailored and professional if it was a corporate office or speaking to the board of directors.

Bohemian if it was left up to me. That was my style, still is.

Clothes are the first message we send. Words follow and sometimes are heard based on the first message. I had great fun with that reality over the years.

When I lived in Austin, Texas, it was part of my professional role to present information before the actual donation segment of a fundraising dinner party. My employers outfitted me in different designer gowns depending on the situation. Following dinner, they would roll out a green chalkboard and, designer dress and all, I would get up and give a mini lecture. The funds we raised were responsible for a great many programs offered to addiction families. Sequins and sassy! We did good!

"Life is too short to wear "boring clothes."
—Sharon Cruse

"Clothes aren't going to change the world,
but the women who wear them will.
—Anne Klein

Putting Your Best Cowgirl Boot Forward

I was fortunate to have been chosen to be the opening speaker at a national conference of 500 doctors and psychiatrists held in Austin, Texas. Intimidating and exciting all at the same time, I was also looking forward to seeing a good friend of mine there, who was also speaking. She loved Country Western dancing and, we arranged to go line dancing at the Broken Spoke. I packed my clothes in a checked suitcase but decided to wear my navy-blue cowboy boots with lizard inserts and my cowgirl hat with pheasant feathers on the airplane because there was no way to pack those two items.

Coming up from the booth area of the conference, I saw the room of the opening presentation and it was already starting to fill. There was just enough time to get ready, grab my materials, and show up for the introductions.

Imagine my horror when I got to my room and found out my luggage had been lost somewhere in transit after we left the airport and was on a shuttle somewhere in Austin. I had noticed that this was maybe one of the most conservatively dressed groups I had addressed in a long time. After a half hour of frantically trying to find my luggage, there was nothing to do, but show up as the guest speaker, wearing my blue jeans, and looking like I was right off the ranch.

On the arm of my host. I started at the back of the room and walked down a red carpet. My heart pounded as I walked behind the podium. I took off   my   hat, placed it on the chair next to the podium. I never explained and never mentioned the way I was dressed. Afterward, I was relieved to get a standing ovation. I picked up my hat and did the customary visiting with people from the audience and then left the building. No one ever mentioned my outfit. Later on, I had a fun-filled night at the Broken Spoke—where I was already totally appropriately dressed for the occasion.

> **"Boots, class, and a little sass.**
> **That's what cowgirls are made of".**
> —Unknown

> **"There is an opportunity and handicap**
> **in every situation."**
> —Virginia Satir

Dapper, Intriguing and Fun

I was the serious one in my marriage. I made appointments, kept the schedules, and responded to RSVPs. Mind you, Joe did his share, but nevertheless, I made things a responsibility and he made things fun. It seemed to be in our natures. Somehow, there was no way not to fall in love with this man's spontaneity, sophistication, and charm. For those of you who have ever lived in an arena of long gowns, formal dinners, and expectations, you know that for a woman to go to a formal dinner, it usually means planning what you are wearing ahead of time, getting your nails and hair done, and all the other preparations. Your husband gets to put on a tux and can shower an hour before the event starts. He looks sharp, and Joe always did. When I saw him in a white tux, tails, a top hat, and white tap shoes, he took my breath away. He always had the charm to do that.

We also did a fair amount of cruising. Today's ships make great accommodations for younger people and families, but the older classic ships still require some sort of formal attire. On one of our cruises, I left for our room early in the afternoon to begin preparations for our formal night. Joe said he was going to visit with a friend and would be up in a few minutes to prepare. I went through the routine and sometime later was ready to go down to dinner. Joe hadn't come back yet. I tried to call, no answer, and I waited until table reservation time and went down to the dining room alone. I was seated with another couple and waited.

About forty-five minutes later, in rushed Joe, breathless, in the same clothes he had worn all day. He was so excited and happy as he told the story of meeting a delightful couple at happy hour, getting to know them, going to the captain's quarters, and being the best man in a last-minute cruise wedding ceremony. He had just finished the service. He held us all captive with his story and was dapper, intriguing, and fun—and nobody noticed he hadn't "dressed" for the formal night. No wonder I loved being with him.

"Relationships are mostly stronger when you are "best friends" first and lovers and a couple later."
—Sharon Cruse

Wine for Grandma

Our first trip to Disney World with our grandchildren, Melanie and Matt, two toddlers, was an experience. I'm still astounded that my daughters trusted us with their little ones for two weeks with their children. The first night we were exhausted after flying, navigating the shuttle buses, and checking in to the hotel. Joe and I crawled into bed after tucking the kids in for the night, or so we thought. An hour later, Matt was standing by the door saying, "I'm ready to go home now." His anxiety was great, and we tried our best to soothe him. It was now midnight, and we were addressing his fear by drawing a calendar on the wall showing him the fourteen days until we were leaving. That helped him to understand that we wouldn't be gone forever, and we all got to go back to bed. We did those two weeks without regret, but it took months to recover from fear, exhaustion, excitement, and joy. By the time they were five, almost six, we were ready to try again.

We were in the Disney World castle and Belle from Beauty and the Beast was enchanting us all. Melanie and Matt were in the front row. By now, we had added two more: Christopher and Ryan. Belle was in the middle of her story about Little Red Riding Hood, and everyone was listening carefully. The tension grew and the story got closer to Grandma's house. Grandpa, of course, was there with the movie camera taping everyone's expressions and emotion. Belle increased her tension with the story and finally said, "We are all close to Grandma's house and we need to bring her a present. What would each of you bring to grandma?Let's all take gifts to Grandma. What would your grandma like to have?"

One little boy said, "A chocolate sundae." Another said, "A piece of apple pie." Another said, "Fried chicken." My granddaughter raised her hand and when Belle asked her, she replied, "My grandma would like a glass of cold Chardonnay wine." Belle was flustered but smiled really big. She quickly said, "Yes, there are non-alcoholic wines, and we will try to find one for your grandma," and quickly changed the subject as the program moved on. Melanie smiled at me as if to say, "Well done," Grandma. I was speechless, but Belle took over as any pro would and the program moved on.

"Out of the mouths of babes" is often said when a young child says something insightful or knowing."
–Sharon Cruse

"Wine is bottled poetry. Some enjoy it and some don't."
–Robert Louis Stevenson

The Giraffettes

I'd told you early about the Frogettes. Over the years, one beloved lady died and another of the group could not continue the meetings of the original bonded group. We missed them and we decided we needed a new bonding mascot and a new mission. We decided to honor their place in our history and move on to another era. We added the behavior of laughing so hard, it took one's breath away and also, we decided to go to the depths of our shared experiences surrounding illness and death. We chose the giraffe as our new mascot and named ourselves "the Giraffettes." We have continued to try to get together as often as we can and to this day remain the best of friends.

Some ask, why the giraffe? We like to think we aspire to be like a giraffe. The giraffe has one of the biggest hearts of all mammals. It takes a big heart to pump blood all the way from the heart to the head. That can be true for people as well. Hearts care so very much and take in so much that each other feels and, in many ways, takes in the concerns of all peoples.

Also, it can be said that we stick our necks out a whole lot. We seem to be the kind of people who take on causes, work as volunteers, see what needs to be done, and tries to answer the problem of ourselves, each other, our families, and our world in general. It is no wonder that giraffes have such long necks as they have so much to do.

Lastly, with that long neck and a head and brain sitting way above the rest, the giraffe holds great vision. We like to try to have that vision. What is going on now and how does that relate to what went on in the past, and where might we be going in the future?

Vision is a great gift. It is our hope as individuals and as Giraffettes, we might add our heart, our decisions, and our vision to make this world a better place to be. I have many giraffes in my home and hope you have one as well. I hold on to and love my frog and wonder what animal I will add next. It just may be the elephant. It is all knowing, is wise, loves companionship, and never forgets. I think that might be where I am going.

"Lots of people want to ride with you in the limo, but what you want is someone who will take the bus with you when the limo breaks down."
—Oprah Winfrey

Putting Out a Fire in Pink Foam Rollers

My father was a bit judgmental, but also a strong, sensitive, kind and jovial sort of guy in the years I was living at home. He loved to go to bed at night and read comic books. He would entertain himself for hours going into the worlds of Superman, Dick Tracy, Donald Duck, and Archie. He really had a great sense of humor. He took great pride in having our family name sewn in the worker's uniforms and owning his own business. His other source of pride was being the driver of the local fire truck.

My father was part Belgian/French and looked the part. He had beautiful black hair and lots of it. He worked hard, and he loved cold beer. He often drank beer with his lunch, lay down on the couch for an afternoon nap, and then hopped up and went back and worked a busy afternoon. One day, while he was napping, I brought my hot pink hair curlers over to his couch and put them on him. I wanted to surprise him with a new hairdo. I wasn't expecting the fire whistle to go off.

I wasn't in the room when this happened, and my dad jumped up off the couch. ran out the door, hopped in the car and went to the fire department. He had no idea the curlers were in his hair even as he drove the truck and then helped put out the fire. Once the fire was responsibly taken care of, the firemen let him in on the fact he had pink foam curlers in his air. He had naturally curly hair, but they teased him for years about curling his hair every day. Fortunately for me, he was a good sport and also thought it was funny!

"Be the first to be able to laugh at yourself and don't take yourself too seriously".
—John Shufeldt

Love in the Afternoon

My career included educational programs on sexuality as well as programs on family therapy, couples counseling, addiction complications, and many other human development issues. At this time in my career, I carried 16-millimeter films as visual aids for my presentations. My travel outfit was usually a tailored suit, three-inch high heels, and an open canvas shoulder bag with the films and all toiletries.

Back then, the planes were full of businessmen. A woman traveling alone was a bit of a rarity, and on many flights, I was the only woman. Leaving for a flight, getting through the airport, and settling in on the plane was always challenging, but one trip stands out in my mind. Heading out for a one-week workshop, my bags were full of materials and visual aids.

After turning over my shoulder bag to the attendant to hang in the general closet, I settled into my aisle seat and proceeded to put my bag under the seat in from of me. We took off and for some reason, my open-topped canvas bag tipped, and all my visual aids rolled under the seats to the back of the plane. It all happened in an instant and was over before I could possibly stop anything. All three of my films that were in the bag slid under the seats to the back of the airplane. Once we were at altitude, an announcement came over the loudspeaker. "Would the owner of the following films please come to the back of the plane to identify them: *Love in the Afternoon* (how retired folk can revive their sex life): *Learning the Difference Between Sensuality and Sexuality,* and *The Family Trap.*"

It took every bit of courage I could muster to go claim my films. I never again traveled with an open bag!

**"I'm carded for R-rated movies. And I get talked down
to a lot, when I try to go rent a car or buy an airplane
ticket or other stuff adults do."**
−Kristen Bell

Chapter Five
History

Surviving Disaster in the Black Hills

Many have known the devastation of fire, which, like all disasters can take away everything in an instant. We had a home in the Black Hills in South Dakota, built of logs, which also housed many of our professional staff from time to time. Joe and I were home alone, and the staff was at our programs one day when about midafternoon we heard a knock at the door. Two policemen told us we needed to evacuate as a fire was roaring up the road. It looked okay to us, but we said we would comply. We quickly grabbed a few things—papers, photos, and some of our guests' belongings—and by the time we left, the smoke from the fire had obscured the huge wooden sign over our driveway that said "Crestwood." Just a few minutes earlier, it was plain as day, but now we no longer could read it as the fire rolled toward out home. Before we left, we knelt for a few minutes in prayer to give us strength.

We got in our car, drove through smoke and haze, and made it to Rapid City, South Dakota. We registered one of last rooms available at the hotel in our tourist town. For many days, we watched television day and night as the fire tore through our neighborhood. It was only on the news at night that we would learn the state of the fire. We did not know whether or not our home was gone. Finally, officials reported that the fire had been contained, but no vehicles were going to be allowed in the area for some time. Joe and I filled up big gallon drinking water jugs and headed up the road on foot, walking three miles until we reached our area. As we reached the top of the hill, we saw houses burned to the ground, some partially destroyed, and then we saw the logs of our home. The fire came up to five feet around our it, then it stopped. We lost our yard, the fence around our home, and the pillows off the deck. Everything else was intact.

The relief was overwhelming. We walked through rubble, unlocked the door, and went inside. It was just as we left it. We were so grateful that we decided to stay. We had no electricity, no water, and no gas, but we did have a totally full indoor hot tub for eight people. We each got a bucket and kept at bay the small fires outside that kept starting and restarting, and we could fill our toilets.

Logs are sealed in way that wood isn't. When the insurance adjuster came to assess the situation, we didn't even have smoke damage inside. We rebuilt, we replanted, and Crestwood went on to bring joy and comfort to its guests again.

"If you don't go after what you want, you could spend your time settling for what you can get."
−Anonymous

A Blast from the Past

Oleo, S&H Green Stamps, and green and gold glass dishes (glass, not china). If you are old enough to remember using these things, we are probably about the same age.

Today, butter comes in squares, blocks, and plastic tubs. In my day, faux butter came in plastic bags. It was called margarine. Real butter is what my dad would make on Sunday mornings, from cream. It was heavenly on toast, muffins, and veggies. However, we would run out of it toward the end of the week and then we used oleo. It was white, like lard, and you received a little capsule of color. Dropping the capsule in the bag, we would squish it around until it turned yellow, squeeze it out into a dish or tub, and use until Sunday when Dad made the real butter. I can't remember the taste of oleo. It just moistened the toast. Real butter is memorable. Check yours. Is it real?

With today's Amazon shopping and other quick delivery services, it's hard to imagine the S&H Green Stamp way of life. From the late 1800s until the 1980s, the Green Stamps were a reward program connected to merchandise. Grocery stores, retail stores, and drug stores all gave them out, and you would affix them in a little booklet until you gained enough to redeem them for household items from a catalog.

The color green was chosen because it meant "money and prosperity." My family coveted them. They stretched the dollar into more buying ability. They were an enticement to the stores that gave them out because it would bring in consumers. I still have a few in my scrapbooks. Today, they are collectors' items.

Finally, the glass dishes. They were either green or gold, and people collected them. Stores and gas stations would give them out, plate by plate, cup by cup. Choosing which stores were giving which dishes was an event. We chose the gold for our family and my father gave away the green in his business. We acquired a full place setting: plate, saucer, coffee cups and then serving pieces. When it was all put together, we felt we were very "uptown" with our beautiful glass dishes.

Squeezing oleo, pasting Green Stamps in small booklets, and bringing home enough points for a plate held families together. We celebrated the small victories and enjoyed these small pleasures. I don't currently have oleo, a book of Green Stamps (though I have a few of the stamps), or a gold glass dish, but I do still have the family memories and excitement they brought into our lives.

Music, food, clothes, all have a way of bringing memories to mind with the thoughts, feelings and connections that go along with them.

> **"Memories are like gardens.**
> **Regularly tend the pleasant blossoms and**
> **remove the invasive ones."**
> —Linda Fifer Raphs

Life Lessons from Grandma's Bowling Alley and Diner

Main Street in Jasper, Minnesota, was between two and three blocks long. It contained a bank, feed store, town hall, gas station, clothing store, diner, and a pub. In the middle of those businesses was my grandma's bowling alley. Coming through those front doors were primarily the local people who either wanted breakfast, a burger for lunch, or one of Grandma Olson's famous donuts: frosted, sugared, or plain served with a cup of egg coffee. For those who have never heard of it, egg coffee is the best. Before brewing the coffee, crush up a few eggshells and put them in the coffee pot. Let them simmer with the coffee for just a bit. Somehow, the shells draw out the flavor of the coffee beans. Ask any real coffee drinker if they know about eggs shells and they will say, "You bet!"

I loved being there with my grandma, enjoying her food, meeting the townspeople and becoming a real bowling pinsetter.

The bowling alley had big metal frames that came down, set the bowling pins up, and then disappeared into the ceiling again. Each pin weighed 3 pounds, 8 ounces. The frame that set them up was big and heavy. Everything today is automatic, but we actually had to set the pins up on the alley, turn on the machine that straightened them into place, get rid of the machine, and hop up on a ledge to not be hit by the incoming fast-moving bowling bowl. By the time I was ten, I was a good and fast pinsetter.

The banter at the bowling alley was loud, the fellowship was close, and the beer was cold., Walking home late at night beside my grandma, I felt like the luckiest girl in the world. After she finished locking up, she went home where she cared for my grandpa, who was ill. He suffered from some illnesses, and she would make him a late supper and get him settled for the night.

By this time, she had already comforted the young unmarried pregnant girl who only came to the bowling alley diner for a late supper likely because she was too ashamed to come out during the day. She had conveniently forgotten to give out the check to a young man who she knew to be broke. She kept the coffee pot going for the poker players who tied up a booth most of the afternoon, and she made sure her granddaughter was a talented and strong pinsetter.

Spending a day with grandma taught me lessons about community building and values that there was no other way to learn. I tried to become more like her with each visit.

By middle high school and high school, my friends were asking me if they could come work in the diner and the bowling alley. They wanted some of my grandma's burgers, donuts, and her unconditional love.

> **"The best classroom in the world is at the feet of an older person."**
> —Andy Rooney

> **"Become the hero/heroine of your own life."**
> —Nora Ephron

Brass Beds, Prophets, and My Heavenly Telephone System

When I was growing up, I slept in an authentic brass bed. If you can imagine, picture a headboard that has many small round holes that were part of the brass of the entire headboard. From the time I was very young, in grade school, I knew there was a God and spiritual power of some kind, and also saints and holy people who had lived.

Although I went to Catholic School, that's not where I learned about God. Instead, I learned that when I made a prayer, things could and did happen as a result, so prayer became an important value for me.

Later, as I learned about the work of telephone operators, it seemed like a good idea to use the small-town telephone system to help me connect with God. Watching the local operators pull up the cords and plug them into the main connection board gave me an idea. I figured that I could tie yellow pencils each to a cord and plug them into the holes on my headboard. When I wanted to talk to God, I could simply pull up a pencil. This gave me a connection that felt real to me.

Many long nights, these cords connected me with God and with special angels (such as St. Francis, St. Jude, and St. Anthony). It was comforting to believe that I had this direct connection anytime I wanted.

Later in life, as part of expanding my belief system, it was clear that God often used broken and or "authentic people" to deliver life-changing messages, it propelled me into following the work of Martin Luther King, Jr., Barack Obama, and Gloria Steinem. My grown-up knowing is how to seek and follow modern-day prophets. Adding to my list of prophets are Eleanor Roosevelt, Mother Teresa, Nelson Mandela, Rosa Parks, John F. Kennedy, Helen Keller, Winston Churchill, Hillary and Bill Clinton. I remain grateful to have learned that there are great teachers who are inspired and maybe still a little broken, but I love to investigate, appreciate, and aspire to that kind of sharing.

"Prayer is the world's greatest wireless connection."
—Sharon Cruse

"Prayer is when you 'talk to God.' Meditation is when you listen to God."
—Joey Reiman and Diana Robinson

"Sometimes God says 'yes,' sometimes 'no' and sometimes 'later.' "
—Sharon Cruse

Freedom Fest 1976

The first time I had a chance to meet the great Dick Van Dyke in person was when he came to visit my new counseling center in Minnesota. He walked in and, true to form, tripped over the footstool. He was up in about ten seconds, holding out his hand, and saying, "Hello, I'm Dick Van Dyke." That was the start of a fun afternoon.

A couple of days earlier, I had seen him from afar in Blooming-
ton, Minnesota, as he hosted the gathering of over 26,000 recovering
alcoholics and their families. Imagine the largest shopping center in
the world at that time, filled with that much recovery and joy. It was
a rainy day, and Dick walked up to the microphone and said, "This is
the wettest bunch of drys I have ever seen." It was, indeed, and we had
gathered to show hope and promise to the thousands who had chosen
recovery over addiction. It is still the largest recovery advocacy group
that has ever gathered in history. It was the result of months of planning and preparation, and the deluge started right before we were
set to begin the event. Nevertheless, we marched into the stadium,
through the rain, getting soaked, and the show carried on. Nothing could stop Minnesotans and the recovery momentum that had
been building through twelve-step programs, twenty-six residential
treatment programs, family counseling centers, employee assistance
programs, and public awareness.

Today, addiction and the treatment of addiction and the power
of AA groups is a more open topic, but in those days, addiction was
taboo and only talked about in hushed tones. There was still shame
attached. Yet, in Minnesota in countless programs and groups, we
had come to know that people can do recover from addiction.
Clearly, alcoholics are intelligent, productive, and talented,
but sometimes have an illness that needs to be managed.

To be there was to be a part of history. Now that our nation
has millions of people in recovery, it is valuable to look back
and honor and celebrate the first men and women and young
people who stepped into the public light to share their experience,
strength, and hope with the world. at The
Freedom Fest, Minnesota, 1976.

**"You must become the change you
wish to see in the world."**
—Gandhi

"Study the past should you want to define the future."
—Confucius

Hundred-Mile Journey

As a young woman working a forty-hour workweek as a secretary in a large firm (Super Valu Stores), I was tired and ready for the weekend. What it meant most Friday nights was that I put gas in my car and started my journey 100 miles to my family home in southern Minnesota. My week in the city was over and I longed for the comfort of my childhood home, my bed, my mom's cooking and the network of people I knew and loved. I was still just seventeen years old. Most of my friends had either left or were leaving for college, but my immediate family and my aunt and uncle were still in my town.

Leaving home five days after graduation and going to work in the city, Minneapolis. was a jolt for me. However, good wages and health and life insurance were benefits I wasn't getting at home, and it seemed to me it was time for me to take responsibility for myself. My parents were struggling. Living with another aunt and uncle made this change possible and helped with the transition. I never returned home again to live—only for visits. For the first two years after high school graduation, the long journey was a weekly happening.

The hundred miles became my connection between worlds. One world was familiar and easy and safe. I knew basically everyone, and everyone knew me. It was my place and there was a sense of truly belonging to my family, my friends, my relatives, and the town. Eventually, that sense of belonging was inside me and gave me confidence and comfort and has stayed with me all my life. The other end of the hundred miles was strange, inviting and offering possibilities that were different from my experience. A sense of new, expansive horizons seems to be constantly appearing out of nowhere. Sometimes, my footing wasn't sure, and I treaded lightly. Sometimes, l took a few steps backward, but mostly the movement was forward, and my life has unfolded in magical ways. I was grateful for the chance to live in two worlds, a hundred miles apart.

"I don't know where I am going but I'm on my way."
—Unknown

The Imperial Inn

I was between residences in two cities and had just moved to Rapid City, South Dakota. Leaving the setting where my beautiful peaceful retreats had become very popular, I was in search of a new setting to help people start the journey to bring inner peace and comfort into their lives. Having had pre-registration of around thirty people in the program in two weeks' time, I knew I had to find something fast and was sure it would happen. However, two weeks of frantic searching turned up nothing. The registrants had all paid air fare and made arrangements to arrive on a Sunday night in Rapid City for a program they had signed up for in advance. (Our move had taken some twists and turns - or it would have been all set).

It was now five days before the first night of the program. We were desperate when someone told me of a motel in downtown Rapid City called The Imperial Inn, so we checked it out. The Inn had a large conference room on the lower level, and we could rent it for the eight days we needed it. We signed on the dotted line and the first program was set up for thirty people and eight staff members.

Opening night, the participants arrived and checked in. We all sat in a very large circle, ready to give names, make new friends, and share addiction issues, hoping for the start of new healing. Above us, the bar belted out loud Country Western music. No one had told us about the bar situated directly above the conference room. We had no choice, of course, we had to go on because this was our only option.

We finished those eight days and people found what they came for. They had been searching for courage, patience, acceptance and letting go. We were practicing what we were teaching. Due to circumstances, we also had an experience that came along with the lectures. We accepted, we found courage to go on, we needed to find endless patience, and we had to let go. We completed six programs there before we found our home. Our new home was exactly the opposite kind of story and more will be revealed in another story. Funny how we teach what we need to learn

**"Things turn out best for the people
who make the best of how things turn out."**
—Art Linkletter

**"Life is 10 percent of what happens to you and
90 percent of how you react to it."**
—Charles R. Swindoll

Jasper Stone Company Legacy

Rock, in general, and especially Jasper rock is an important part of my story. As I've said, my grandma owned a rooming house and a bowling alley in Jasper. My stays in the rooming house and my hours at the bowling alley shaped my young thoughts and street smarts. The rooming house was filled with boarders (stonecutters from Scotland) who quarried the stone. The town was named after the red quartzite that is quarried there. Many buildings have been built from Jasper rock and it is used in many parts of the country for making headstones. It put the town on the map as it exported rock. At this time, it's still a small town and if one wants to walk through history, Jasper is a good place to start. Some parts of the quarry are working to this day. The quarry of course, brought the railroad to Jasper and, eventually, my grandma who worked at the beanery (railroad restaurant). The small town of around 500 people was established in the 1800s.

I am the oldest living person in the Rae clan. My name is Sharon Rae.

Imagine, my grandma, a woman in the 1940s, supporting her family of four. (Had been five, but one child died). She also informally adopted a boy and girl whose parents were killed in an auto accident. She raised them as well. Her husband was disabled, and she supported the family. Between the bowling alley, the restaurant, the rooming house, and the beanery, my childhood was filled with people, good food, strong women and an example that anything was possible. I loved my time in Jasper, and even after my family moved away, I returned to spend summers, and vacations there and invited my girlfriends to travel with me. Everyone wanted to go with me to Jasper, Minnesota.

It was a quintessential small Midwestern town, and as John F. Kennedy once said, "History is a relentless master. It has no present, only the past rushing into the future." Dr. Suess wrote the book *Oh, the Places You Will Go*, which was certainly prophetic for me. If Grandma were alive today, she would be so excited and happy that Jasper still lives within me. I hope I will return and visit someday, but if that doesn't happen, it's all alive and well today, sitting on my fireplace in three forms at this very moment. A rough piece, a pebble just quarried, and a finished product. How exciting is that and I look and remember my years in that Midwestern town.

I am proud to be a descendant of the Rae family of Scotland, who set down roots in Jasper. Rock is important to me.

"Rocks are not lifeless; they resonate with a memory that is the very essence of life itself."
—When Earth Speaks

Stalked by a Stranger

We lived in a friendly, quiet upscale neighborhood in the suburbs in a beautiful two-story house that had a pond behind it. There was even a treehouse for the kids to play in. It felt serene and safe.

As a young mother, my days were busy. Sometimes, the house didn't get a quick once-over cleaning until all the toys were put away and my three children were sound asleep. Running through the house, doing last-minute clean-up and sometimes shaking out the rugs was something I did in the evening, usually after dark. My husband worked into the evening on Friday nights, but I never thought twice about it. After all, this was a safe place . . . or so I thought.

One night, while I was shaking out the rugs, a deep, male voice came from up in the treehouse. "I've been watching you." I was surprised at first, then felt blood-curdling fear as I ran back into the house and locked the door. My heart pounded as I waited for the sound of my husband's key in the door lock. It was forty-five minutes but felt like an eternity.

This was just the beginning of my stalking nightmare. Often, it happened in broad daylight. While having a cup of coffee with a friend one day, my phone rang. I answered it and heard the same deep male voice from the treehouse on the other end. He said, "Have a good coffee." We had notified the police, of course, and they often kept a car nearby, but the stalker never tipped his hand.

Later, another neighbor started receiving surprise visits and calls as well. The police gave us both small handguns and suggested we keep them close. I was as afraid of the gun as the stalker and put it on the highest shelf in my dining room with the gun and bullets separated.

One day at about four o'clock in the afternoon, with the children in the family room, I went out on our porch and there he was watching through the screen door. I screamed, ran inside, and locked the door. Then I ran to the entry door and slammed and locked it as I saw him round the house. I called the police and waited for them, holding my children close. About fifteen minutes later, I heard a gunshot and soon the police were at the door. The man had tried to enter the neighbor's house and the neighbor shot him. He had been fatally wounded. No one knew him and, thankfully, the stalking stopped. Fifty years later, my heart still pounds when I remember that six weeks of terror. After that, we never had another treehouse. Fear is powerful and builds a home inside us.

"Stalking is not normal behavior. In person or cyber. It shows a person without boundaries, a shaky grasp on reality and mental illness tendencies."
—Dr. Maxine Stockwell

Nurturing Networks

In the 1970s, I taught a class in human resources at the University of Minnesota Public Health Department. The students loved my extensive handouts. The class was popular, so we added another class and then another. The handouts were getting expensive since there were now so many students. At the time, my son was in college and my two girls and I lived together.

With money tight and expenses high making all these handouts, I decided to maybe write them, get them printed, and sell them for cost. In order to do that, I needed to incorporate as a small business and hire my high school aged daughters to help me. I incorporated as "Nurturing Networks" and was soon in business. I hired an accountant and a lawyer, and we were on our way. My son researched and helped us by making our first investment, which was Kaypro computer—one of the early brands of computer. My daughters learned that by changing their voices around, they could become our different department employees. Between the four of us, we had an order department, distribution center, mail room, and customer service. I wrote the first booklets, and we were in business. The year was 1972. We applied for a bulk mailing permit and set up a mail center using brown paper bags (marked A–Z) in our living room. We became mail order only. We also copyrighted everything that I wrote. We started out selling a minimum of ten booklets on each topic. Imagine our surprise when the orders started coming in by the thousands. We used my portable typewriter in the beginning and then the Kaypro with pages stapled at the center. The increased volume meant we had to move to a local print shop.

Eventually, I took those early booklets, put them together, and published my first hard-cover book, which became a bestseller and in 1982 won The Marty Mann Award for the best communication in the field of addiction. The book eventually became a 16-millimeter film, which also won many awards. Today, that book and the film are still involved in most treatment centers and many mental health centers.

Eventually, a company to carry forth the message and offer onsite treatment was founded in 1978 and still exists today in Cumberland Furnace, Tennessee. Today, it is called Onsite Workshops.

A mother and two daughters with a mission and one son offering his skills and working out of a living room grew into a publishing company and a training/treatment center. The rest is history as the work is turning global.

"You don't sit down and wait for opportunities to come. Get up and make them."
—Madame C. J. Walker

Onsite Workshops

It all started when I began putting together groups of children whose parents were clients in my counseling programs. Bringing them joy, through fun ideas and music was very important to me. I was helping their parents with issues of addiction in one way or another. To me, it felt like their children could use some special time and attention. My first agency was founded in 1973, and I called it the Family Factory. Without funds or startup money, we accepted a building that an H & R Block owner offered up for free from May to January (outside of tax season). There was connection, group therapy, music, and lectures. Programs were about $10.00 a month and all group leaders were volunteers.

The League of Women Voters, church groups, community volunteers and friends of mine offered to be the group leaders and presenters. By the end of the summer of 1973, we had around 200 children, under the age of 17, regularly coming to these groups. Even my children helped to lead groups (if they were older than the group members). *The Minneapolis Star-Tribune* newspaper did an article about these efforts in their Sunday edition.

I was then called by a minister who had read the article and offered us a three-story house sitting near his Lutheran church, also in Minneapolis. Our program was able to expand and just breathe more deeply. We had space, and it was wonderful. Dick Van Dyke was in Minneapolis for another function I was involved in, and he was interested in children of alcoholics. He attended our opening.

It was a grand experience. We called this agency The House. We continued our work at the agency until I was offered a position as a program developer and intervention trainer for a non-profit agency called "The Johnson Institute," developer of the Minnesota Model of intervention.

My belief was that if we paid attention to the family of the alcoholic, intervention would work sooner and better. I accepted the role of developing a family intervention model and my agency, The House, grew into the Family Care Department of The Johnson Institute. While working there, the family model was accepted and through our training programs moved across the model. It was the beginning of family treatment for alcoholic families and morphed into help for all dysfunctional family systems.

By 1978, I had learned two things. The first was that family therapy experiential therapy worked better than singular talk therapy. I also felt that the hoops and paperwork necessary for a non-profit company was too demanding and wasteful, and I decided to start my own business—one that would be for-profit and family-based. That program began in 1978. I incorporated as The Center for the Development of Human Potential. I continued to add alternate therapies and programs and had the option to experience. For-profit agencies have much more leadership ability than non-profit models. The demand for my model spread to the military (primarily the Air Force, corporations (including United Airlines, Burlington Northern Railway, Pillsbury, and General Mills). Two happenings converged. I was traveling onsite delivering training in my model and the receptionist was tired of using our long name when she answered the phone. I reincorporated at that time, changing from The Center for the Development of Human Potential to Onsite Treatment and Training.

Onsite continues to bring hope and help to this day. It is located in Tennessee and only changed the name a tad. It's now known as Onsite Workshops. The Onsite work lives in my heart. It has had only three custodians, and it was my honor was to be the first.

> **"The best way to predict the**
> **future is to create it."**
> —Abraham Lincoln

Minneapolis Lakers

As the oldest child in a family who liked to socialize, I often was assigned the job of cleaning up after Sunday dinner parties, where the adults drank, smoked, and talked. My refuge became listening to the radio and the Minneapolis Lakers, the professional basketball team that began in Minnesota, long before moving to Los Angeles. This made a very big impression on me. They were a great team and so skilled. As a small-town farming community teen, I reveled in their skills and knew the scores of the game and the standing of the team at all times.

Every Sunday night they played at home in Minnesota. When I turned sixteen, I started driving my uncle's car to Minneapolis (about

100 miles away) and would take a friend along, to attend the home games. The whole event took many hours, but rarely did I miss a home game. My parents didn't think anything about a sixteen-year-old driving into a big city, finding the game, and driving home in the middle of the night. At 8 o'clock on Monday morning, I was back in school—and usually very tired.

I kept scrapbooks and newspaper clippings. What a thrill when I was visiting a Minneapolis aunt and uncle to find out, through an article, that they lived near Jim Pollard, who was a starter on the team. As soon as I could, I went out walking, determined to find his house, and I did. I didn't just find his house, I went up and knocked on the door, determined to meet him. To my amazement, he answered the door. I was shocked at how tall he was in person. He called for his wife, and she invited me to come in. I shared my story. He, in turn, called George Miken, the famous center and also on the starting team. They were joined by Dugie Martin, Whitey Skoog, and Joey Hutton. I thought I had died and gone to heaven. Eventually, through friendship and being a big fan, I donated all my scrapbooks to Jim Pollard and his family.

The Minneapolis Lakers were an important part of my high school experience. Meeting them all in person and getting to know them was a highlight.

**"I've failed over and over again in my life . . .
and that's why I succeed."**
–Michael Jordon

**"One man can be a crucial ingredient on a team,
but one man can't make a team".**
–Kareem Abdul-Jabbar

Minnesota North Stars Hockey

My friend, a counseling psychologist called me one day with an interesting offer. He had a friend who was a partner in owning the Minnesota North Stars hockey team. This friend had a friend who was the chairman of the board of my company. The two owners wanted me and my friend to come in and meet with the owners of the North Stars and the players because they were stuck at the bottom of the league. They were all good players, so why was this happening? We agreed to become consultants.

The first time we met with the owners, all went quite well and there was plenty of leadership, good hiring, and great intentions, but the team spirit was still flat. At first, the team looked both of us counselors over and snickered. They weren't really interested in meeting with what they referred to as "shrinks." After a few days of non-interest, my friend asked if he could skate with them. After a few chuckles, they agreed. Little did they know that my friend was an outstanding Canadian hockey player and being a psychologist was a backup career. Once the players realized he was one of them, we were given respect.

After a few sessions, we concluded the issue wasn't with the owners and began investigating the players. What we learned after a few sessions over several months was that the team was doing "pillow talk." No matter how well the team was performing, there seemed to be angst on the ice. They were fouling each other out and our challenge was to find out what was happening. We also asked to meet with the hockey wives. Therein we found the problem.

There were older, seasoned hockey wives and newer hockey wives and girlfriends. The older hockey wives were willing and trained to follow their husbands around to new locales, raise the children, and keep the home fires burning. The newer hockey wives and girlfriends were a different group of women. They wanted to travel with the players. They liked the big cash incentives. They were willing Ito postpone having children. Each had different ways of being a "hockey wife." They shared with their husbands these different lifestyles, and any angst they had came out between the men on the ice. However, each group longed for some of what the other group had going for them. We encouraged the wives to talk to each other and share their experience, hopes, and lifestyle with one another and to learn something from the other group's lifestyle. They began to share more. We had them meet in groups and learn from one another. As they did so, they shared their new thoughts and attitudes with their husbands (more pillow talk) and fortunately for all, playing hockey became the main focus again for the North Stars. The team won the Stanley Cup in 1999, and they made it to the finals five different times.

Never underestimate the power of learning from each other or the far-reaching effects of that learning.

"Hockey is a special sport in the sense that you need each other pulling in the same direction in order to be successful."
—Wayne Gretsky

Murder on the 10th Floor

A woman traveling alone can never be too cautious. I was attending a conference on addiction at which I was to deliver a training session. After enjoying a dinner with the conference owner at the Antlers Hotel the night before the event started, I went to my room to prepare the opening presentation of the conference the next day. I had settled in for the evening and, as per my usual instruction to the front desk,

I was expecting no one and didn't want phone calls. I was in my "get in the zone" mood. Early in the evening, there was knock at my door and a note under the doorway. It said, "room service." I didn't answer the door. Following a long, hot bath, there was another knock at my door. Again, another room service note was slid under the door. At that point, I called the front desk and then room service. They assured me they hadn't sent any room service to my room. I asked security to check the area and my room in particular. They assured me that all was well. I went to bed.

There were noises in the hallway during the night, but I was tired after my flight and quickly went back to sleep. Imagine my shock in the morning when I discovered that my room had been blocked off and policemen were patrolling the hallways. I immediately went back to my room, locked the door, and called the front desk. A woman had been raped and murdered at the hotel. She was found that morning. And it all happened on my floor. Heart pounding, I left with a security person who took me to the auditorium to deliver the opening presentation to about 200 people. We had to navigate through police, newspaper reporters, TV cameras, and chaos. It was quite an unsettling experience.

The case went unsolved for forty years until a man was ultimately arrested for the rape and murder. Remembering the knocks on my door and the notes stating "food service'" when it hadn't been ordered now made some kind of terrifying sense. I was very happy that my personal choice was that I never answered my hotel/motel door when traveling, and I always gave a code word to room service.

"A useful maximum, 'Two rarities combined call for close attention.'"
—Robert Jordon

My Semi-Nomadic Life

The 2021 movie *Nomadland* won many awards. It told the story of people who travel the country in vans, living a nomadic lifestyle. It revealed a life that more people than we realize have chosen. Some people stay rooted in one place their whole lives. Others, like those featured in the film, move around and have no one place to call home. Each group has their reasons. There is no right and wrong.

I attach myself and like to collect mementos of my life and the places I have lived and visited. Someone recently mentioned, "I love coming to your house because, in many ways, it's like a museum."

My roots are in Minnesota but, like a tree, my branches have grown out and started new roots. It's one of the things I like about myself.

New roots have taken place as I have lived and explored the lifestyles of open farmland in Minnesota, the city of Minneapolis, Minnesota, the Southwestern culture of Austin, Texas. The move from Texas bought me to Palm Springs, California, for a short time. Then the hills of South Dakota called my name, and I entered a time of learning about, native populations, especially the Lakota Sioux. While there, the tug of the Midwest called me back to small-town living in Marine on St. Croix, Minnesota. Many times, to follow my longings and cravings, I lived in two homes at the same time.

The longest time in one area was a cross between forty years in Minnesota, twenty years in Las Vegas, and twelve years in the Black Hills of South Dakota. Most of the time, I was living in two parts of the country at one time.

As a couple and as a family, we all took part in the richness of these culture meccas. What can you say about Minnesota and Minnesota nice? It was a wonderful place—you betcha! It is a part of my stoic and deeply valued heritage. The Black Hills of South Dakota taught me diversity, solitude, and the beauty of the land. Las Vegas was the best part of every vacation (good food, entertainment, and hospitality.

In the current chapter of my life, I am living in Colorado. It seems to me that Colorado is a little bit of all the places I have called home. It's like a summary statement and it comforts me and keeps me connected with all facets of my life. What I know for sure is that it would have been a good investment in my life to have bought stock in a moving company!

"We must be willing to let go of the life we've planned, so as to have the life that is waiting for us."
—Joseph Campbell

Radio Magic

People don't sit around and listen to the radio much in today's culture. It hasn't always been that way. Years ago, for most families, the radio was the center of all connection to the world. There were, of course, newspapers, but it was the radio that brought all ages, all peoples, together to learn about big news, war, and major catastrophes. In today's culture the only radio experience many have is in the car; most of the time used for listening to music, sometimes used for news. Radio shows on National Public Radio (NPR) is a favorite of mine. An FM station that plays easy listening classic music is also a daily experience for me.

Perhaps the best radio for me has been Garrison Keillor's *Prairie Home Companion*. It was my weekly treat for years and years and it was the one show I tried to never miss. Dinners out, Saturday night gatherings, and family events needed to be planned around the weekly radio show. His pulling together some of the best musicians and artists was genius and masterful. Many around the country listened as he wove story after story together like the director of a great and classic film. We all visited home in our minds as he bridged from subject to subject.

As a young girl, I followed the romantic radio stories that were also broadcast weekly. These soap operas were invited into the homes of young girls like me. We were finding our way and these shows provided dreams, conflicts, and victories for young minds: *Helen Trent, Our Gal Sunday* and many more.

Later in life, the radio took me through many adventures by meeting and following professional basketball. Radio opened new worlds for those of us who grew up in rural areas. Today, in my apartment the computer dominates, and televisions have a role, Amazon is a wonderful resource, but my Bose radio brings me joy, news and classical music. For me, it wouldn't be the same connected and wonderful world without it. Come back, Garrison Keillor, I miss you, and I do wonder what ever happened to Helen Trent? I do know that the radio show aired over 7,000 episodes. But the bigger questions was, what did happen to *Our Gal Sunday?*" Did this girl from a little mining town in the West find happiness as the wife of a titled Englishman?

"Radio news is bearable. This is due to the fact that while the news is being broadcast, the disk jockey is not allowed to talk."
—Fran Lebowitz

The Thrill of My First Car

For years, the tin coffee cans hidden in the abandoned heat pipes of my house contained my loose change: most often quarters earned by day work. I turned sixteen, and the plans was to buy my first car and pay for it myself. I didn't even think about insurance and am sure I never had it.

I spent many hours at my uncle's farm, pulling mustard for half a day to earn two quarters. Babysitting brought two and sometimes three quarters. The cans were filling up. It was quite a victory that, when my sixteenth birthday finally came, I was ready to take my driver's test and buy my first car.

The test was in New Ulm, Minnesota. On that particular birthday there was also a bit of a snowstorm and the bureau where I had to take the exam was thirty-five miles away, but I was determined. The written test was no problem. Pulling out of the testing site, with the testing examiner beside me, I started down the chosen street. It was still snowing. Suddenly, I heard a thud and saw a person up on my hood. Yes, I had hit someone. There was lots of commotion. Applying the brakes, the examiner was on it. He got back into the car and said, "Carry on." I did, and when we arrived back at the test site, I was sure I had failed. Imagine my surprise when he said, "You passed with an 88 out of 100." Not only did I pass, but with flying colors since 75 was the fail number. I came to find out that the person on my hood had caused the accident and was not hurt. The examiner said I handled it perfectly and the only part I failed was parallel parking.

By Monday of the next week, my dad and I choose a black Studebaker. I paid for it in quarters. I bought ter- rycloth seat covers and dyed them in my mother 's washing machine (another whole story) and the color was hot pink. The car came with Venetian blinds in the windows. I then hung a pair of dice on the rearview mirror. I was ready to go. It was, as the song goes, "A Moment to Remember."

"The cars we drive say a lot about us."
—Alexander Paul

Telephone Operator: Connecting Us to the World

Nearly everyone has a cell phone these days, and they are usually close at hand, but it still isn't as exciting as the corded phone either on the wall or the desk of my growing-up years. It was black and always commanded attention. When it rang, everyone was a bit startled, and the whole family shared one. If you were out and about and needed to call someone, you had to find a public phone or ask someone if you could use the one in their home or business. If you were driving in your car, you had to find a phone booth, built and designed to simply hold a phone. It operated on a cash basis, and you had to either have the money to deposit into the phone or you had to call "collect," which meant the person who received the call had to accept the charges. Making and receiving a phone call was a big deal. You considered how much cash you had, how much you would need to spend on the call and how to get it done. If you called someone "out of town," there were special charges for the long-distance call, which had variable rates on the time of day—later at night was less expensive.

All this process had to work somehow, and in the early days was facilitated by a telephone operator. Imagine a large brass board with holes punched in it. The holes would be the diameter of a pencil, then each pencil-like stick, which had a long cord on it that was connected to a machine that received the call. The telephone operator would pick up a stick when a call rang and ask what number you wanted. Each little call was assigned a number. She sought out the number, put the stick into the corresponding hole and the two callers were connected through the cord. Our family number was 32117.

Other than making the call, or receiving a call, the most fun was to go to the operator's office and watch the amazing process. Many times after school, I would go to the operator's office just to marvel at the process. People who were not together were talking together and that felt like a miracle.

To save money, families would all use one cord, and it was called a "party line." It was much cheaper than a private line. The way you could tell your call from another call was that you had your own ringtone. Ours was two shorts, a long, and a short. If you heard a call come in and it wasn't your ring, you were alerted that it was someone else's call, and you could ignore it. On a boring day, you could pick it up, stay very quiet, and listen in to other peoples' calls. Life around the telephone office was an exciting life.

Some of you may remember Lily Tomlin, who had a recurring role as Ernestine the telephone operator on the *Laugh In* television show. She had to have spent some of the same hours I did with the telephone operator. She had it down pat!

"In the business world, an executive knows something about everything, a technician knows everything about something, and the switchboard operator knows everything."
—Harold Cohen

The Fire That Changed Our Lives

Living in my small town was a gift because we all knew each other. My deep roots involved the Catholic grade school, and Catholic culture in town, where we had a large and new Catholic church. The other cultures were Minnesota Scandinavians, farmers, and townspeople. My personal history was Catholic, a mixture of French, Scottish, and Norwegian, and a townsperson.

My father, who raised himself to adulthood after he was orphaned at eight, worked up to building and owning a first little shopping center. It was a long and hard road from living with different farm families over the years.

It was quite an accomplishment for him to build his business from the ground up. The center of his shopping center was a chicken hatchery and business. It involved having farmers bring their eggs in, he incubated them for three weeks, and every Monday morning hatched about 500 chickens. My job was helping count them and sort them every Monday night. I was about ten when I was entrusted with this job. He eventually added a Zenith radio shop, a Norge appliance store, a gas station, and a feed store. It quickly became the hub in our little town. There were really three hubs: the Catholic church, my father's shopping center, and the grain elevator. Life was good.

One frigid night in January when the thermometer read 10 degrees below zero, we were awakened by explosions and a flashing red light. I was about fifteen years old. We lived across the street from the hatchery and shopping center. We were horrified to see it erupting in flames. Firemen battled to try and find water and manage the frigid weather, but it was so cold the fire hydrants were frozen. We all worked to keep the firemen from freezing their hands. It was a mix of chaos and disbelief. My uncle (who was caretaker) lost everything and stood in shock, as we all did, watching the flames destroy what we had worked so hard to build.

By morning, all that was left was ash and rubble. All our lives were changed forever that night.

We were left in financial ruin, which was a combination of inadequate insurance in those days, the 1950s, and the fact that my father didn't have enough business management or money to self-insure. We watched our security, and our dreams burn that night. The townspeople gathered around my father and did their best to get him back in business within a week. Someone loaned a building; some came to physically help set up the building. The huge business of chicken incubators, the physical storehouse of feeds and products could not be duplicated. It would have been too costly. It was a tragedy for the whole town in many ways.

The process of my mom's depression and my dad's suicide years later were partially rooted in that evening. The resiliency my brother, sister, and I demonstrated later in life were also rooted in that night.

An investigation of the fire determined it was caused by arson. One year later, also in January, the grain elevator was burned down—also arson—as was the Catholic church the following year. There was so much loss in our little town. After this, the fires stopped. The arsonist was never found, only his or her materials. Was it a local? Someone from out of town? We never found out and might never know. What I do know is that our little town in the heartland of America kept pulling together and today thrives.

> **"A person who hasn't grieved a significant loss has unfinished busines inside and can cause others great grief as a result."**
> —Henry Cloud

The Grove

On my aunt and uncle's farm was a grove, a cluster of trees where nobody went. As a little girl, maybe about five or six, I started going into it. It was maybe thirty or forty feet from the house and, as I think about it today, no one noticed I was gone. It was my special place. I framed it by putting rocks around an area that I called "my home." There, I had a kitchen, a bedroom, and a sitting room. I would bring an empty can from around the house into my kitchen and pretend to make cookies by mixing dirt and water together. Then I put them on a board and set them in the sun to dry. In the bedroom, I had taken a big towel no one missed, and it became my bed. Sometimes, in this wonderful shade, I fell asleep. In my living room, I rehearsed talks with the friends I planned to make.

My playhouse went on for several seasons. I am not sure when I stopped going to the grove, but I never told anyone about it. As an adult today, I wonder why no one missed me; maybe that's just the way it was in those times. Children were presumed to be safe and busy and seeking their own pastimes, unless a crisis occurred that needed attention.

Over the years, my cookies got fancier with stones and twigs and decorations, my naps got a little longer, and my friends were more available. I treasure those days, when my imagination was free to create and roam. Maybe that time gave me some of the inspiration that I feel today to continue to create and share.

My plan is to return to that farm, that grove, and those times, which were an important part of my growing-up years. As someone who still enjoys solitude, I am grateful for this magical time of childhood. Later, I came to know that the definition of a grove literally means "trees with no undergrowth." It can be a handful or acres. In many spiritual traditions, a grove means "space for a Goddess of Love—secret, separate, and untouchable." That is how I felt as a little girl when I would disappear to go "play in the grove."

**"It was a magical private place to go.
Just me and nature fostering possibility."**
—Sharon Cruse

Chapter Six
Life Lessons

Addiction: A Complicated Subject

People often ask me for a simple description of addiction, but it's a complicated subject and as varied as the people involved. Nevertheless, I will attempt to give two short answers, and, beyond that, we will have to talk . . .

One quick description: "Addiction is using any substance or repeating any behavior over and over despite negative consequences." Chemical addiction includes substances such as alcohol, prescription drugs, illegal drugs, vapor, nicotine, etc. Process addictions include overeating, starving, gambling, exercise, work, sexual activity, and computer done to excess.

A second good description is the addictive process: "A person either ingests a chemical or repeats a behavior to feel better over time. A tolerance to the substance or behavior is created and the person needs to increase the amount or frequency to stay feeling good. Eventually, the person needs the substance or behavior just to feel normal (where they had started).

Addicts, whether on the street or at a high-end cocktail party, all have the same behavior patterns. Addiction is equal opportunity for all races, levels of class, age, sex, and financial status. It has no favorites.

"If you are addicted in one thing, then you are not able to live your life as you like to."
—Sophiya Durai Reddy

Caregiving

Rosalyn Carter said it best: "There are only four kinds of people in the world: Those who have been caregivers, those who are currently caregivers, those who will be caregivers, and those who will need caregivers."

We are all just one step from a lifestyle change: an accident, diagnosis of serious or terminal illness, disability, and the complications from the natural process of aging. People who are caregivers are often called "the invisible workforce."

There are countless people who love someone in their family and come to that person's need. They offer rides, time, holidays, advice, hands-on care, just to name a few. They respond because they care, but it is difficult work, and they often feel like they give and give but it's never enough. It truly isn't ever enough, because of the needs of the person receiving care. Those needs don't go away.

Sometimes, it's necessary to go beyond the family and hire private care, and so a massive professional caregiving field and network has grown up around the fact that people live longer in today's culture and need increasingly intensive care that families often are not able to provide.

Caregiving is important and often holds families together but also sometimes tears them apart. My family has faced several caregiving situations. We have grown. There has been giving and receiving care at different times. Chances are that your family has been touched or will be touched by a similar situation as I noted in my book *Caregiving: Hope and Health for Caregiving Families*.

> **"Maybe life isn't about avoiding the bruises;
> maybe it's about collecting the scars to
> prove we showed up for it."**
> —Hannah Branche

> **"Caring can be learned by all human beings,
> can be worked into the design of every life,
> meeting and individual need as well as
> a pervasive need in society."**
> —Mary Catherine Bateson

Complicated Grief

When my husband died, my grief was overwhelming and very complicated. It felt like he died and a part of me died with him. This statement is true but not true. He didn't die completely.

Only his physical body died. His life lives on through me and everyone who knew and loved him. He made a large imprint and still does. That's part of his immortality. The part of me that died with him is also true. No longer am I part of a couple, no longer is my best friend with me when I need to hear his love for me. Those are lonely times. Memories conquer loneliness, however, and I wouldn't trade those memories or that touch for anything. They are mine. I was his and nothing changes that fact. It's complicated.

My first close encounter with death was losing my closest friend –my grandma. She and I were joined and shared good times, bad times, scary times, and the funnest times in the world. She became old when I was busiest in my life, but we never stopped the fun we had. Losing her was a major loss and one that hurts some today. We loved each other but it was time for her to leave this world. This grief was uncomplicated.

When I lost my father in tragic circumstances, he was only forty-six, and I was not prepared for that death. I had just given birth and was busy with a newborn and a toddler. Emotionally, in his death, I lost my mother as well because she was in raw grief until she died. The fears I felt for my much younger brother and sister was overwhelming. Not only for me, but for everyone, grief was complicated.

Within two weeks of my father 's death, my best girlfriend died. She, too, had a newborn and was my age, twenty-three. This was not supposed to happen. Why did she get cancer so young and why did she leave us? Could a diagnosis bring frightening news and an early death for me, too, or for someone else I knew and loved? It did a few years later with my sister. Grief was complicated.

My mother's death came relatively early. I loved her dearly as she was my mom, but I was never totally sure she and I "liked" each other. Love, yes; like, not as sure. Sometimes mother/daughter relationships are very close and intimate—like mine with my grandma. Sometimes, there is tension, different approaches to life, many different opinions and wants. That was more like my relationship with my mother. Grief was complicated.

> **"Should you shield the valleys from the windstorms, you would never see the beauty of their canyons."**
> —Elisabeth Kübler-Ross

Confidence Conquers

Just what instills in or robs us of personal confidence? Here is one of my struggles! Even though I have countless cookbooks, the internet is abundant with ideas, and although I have cooked thousands of pretty good meals, little instills more anxiety in me than inviting good cooks over for a homemade meal. it seems I always try something too hard, too labor intensive, and, in my opinion, falls short of the expected plan I had originally put together. Usually, confidence isn't a big issue for me.

I had worked on building confidence years earlier. I started speaking to groups in grade school when I began to protest that the Catholic church wouldn't support my becoming a priest because I was a female. I really wanted to be a parish priest. Later in life, becoming a public speaker fulfilled much of need to want to do sermons and my confidence in speaking grew. Entertaining and giving parties became a favorite hobby of mine when I remembered how much entertaining my grandma, my aunts, my daughters, and my sister did without batting an eye. I learned to hostess many great parties, but I often catered the food because I was afraid to cook. My confidence in cooking just didn't happen.

Having such great cooks in my family wasn't helping instill confidence, but slowly, in my own way, I tried a few things. Some worked and some didn't. However, the confidence in cooking just didn't happen and I found that the thing I did best was to collect phone numbers for great catering and delivery services. It continued to bother me that I wasn't the confident cook that most people in my family were.

In life, I've learned that the past holds many secrets and clues to why we are the way we are, so I went searching. I decided to go in my memory bank and find some experiences that shattered my confidence. Then I remembered a favorite dish in my family was pea salad. It was simple, some peas, some cubed cheddar cheese, and chopped up homemade dill pickles, all mixed up with some great cold mayonnaise. It was a salad that went with chicken, ham, or beef. As a young child, making the salad for Sunday dinner was assigned to me. I think I was very, very young and excited to be included in meal preparation in this way. I cut cheese, I chopped pickles, and I put the can of peas in a bowl and mixed it all with mayo. Putting it on the table, I waited with pride to be part of the compliments our family cooking brought. Instead of those words of praise I hoped for, everyone started laughing, a couple even laughed hysterically. I didn't know what was so funny until someone said, "Didn't you know you have to drain the peas?" No, I didn't know this, but it became a "family joke" told and retold about the first time Sharon ever made the family pea salad. It's a funny thing.

Once I conquered the pea salad, my confidence started growing slowly and, today, I have added some specialties to my menu, but there is always a bit of anxiety when I serve others. If you ever try this salad, just be sure to drain the liquid from the can of peas!

"Your success will be determined by your own confidence and fortitude."
—Michelle Obama

Dogs Have Homes—Forever

Dogs have always been part of my family. Brownie was my first. Mom, Dad, and Grandma all insisted on dogs. They are good for the soul, they would say. It was our dog Pepper that pushed into my soul and loved her role as princess. My children all took turns being her best friend. Somedays, I just looked into those big brown eyes and our hearts met and we each understood. My husband, however, decided she was too much work and barked way too often at the neighbors. After a very bad barking spell, he made a rash decision and insisted that Pepper had to go. He said the Humane Society would find her a better home, where she was free to roam and would not have the same "city-need" to bark. Hours of debate with him did not make him change his mind. Pepper had to go.

That decision broke my heart, and I bundled Pepper up in my car along with her dish, her bed, and her toys. I drove her to my farming community 100 miles away, sure that my aunt and uncle would take her to their farm. Upon arriving, they shared that they had two dogs and several cats, and just couldn't take one more animal. Heartbroken, I put Pepper on the back seat and headed to another farm, and then another farm. The stories were all the same. No one wanted Pepper.

Sitting in a motel room, after two tanks of gas so far, she and I watched the stars together and my heart simply said, *No, Pepper needs to go home.* Putting her in the back seat, I headed for Minneapolis. She sat on the back seat, with her chin elevated, and watched out the window, looking like the Princess she was, and jumped out with joy when she saw my children. As my husband realized what had just happened, I simply said, "Pepper is not leaving. This is her home." And our home is where she lived for several more years—as a princess.

"Dogs do speak, but only to those who know how to listen."
—Orthan Pamuk

The Challenges of Downsizing

I've owned thirteen different residences and am now living in a community in a small unit. Learning to downsize has been challenging, especially since history, genealogy, and treasures are my passion and sparks of joy. I still have my baby dish, Grandma's bank book, Dad's ballpoint pen (with his name on it), and my sister's flowerpot. Adding to those items are many of my children's gifts to me and, of course, artwork by two of my grandchildren. What's a genealogist to do?

These decisions are the ones that helped me the most:

When I was living in my last single-family home, I used blue carpenter tape and taped off the area that my husband and I lived in. We found it was a lot smaller area than the overall square footage of our home. We knew we could live in less space if our basic needs were met.

I was then left with what to do with "the stuff." There is a difference between useful stuff, and stuff you love, and all the stuff that doesn't meet either category. The process began. All useless stuff went first. We gave up the phrase, "Someday I might want this." Today is someday and today I don't want it. One measure I used in the beginning is, "Can it be replaced?" Anything that can be replaced isn't a treasure. Treasures are irreplaceable—whether they have a monetary value or not.

Then came the goodbyes. For me, many things had served me well. And I said goodbye to that chair, to that coat, and to that dish. I kept in mind all the people who were going to be happy because my things were going to their homes. I began to sell, to consign, to give away, and to toss. With each release, it felt like I lost pounds and baggage. Literally, I gave away all but one one chest, two small tables, a few suitcases, and memory treasures. If it takes more than that, I'm not going anyway.

Then I wrote down: what did I keep, why did I keep it, and would I prefer it goes from here. Granted, I won't be dispensing my treasures after I am gone, but it will be easier for others than it has been for me to let go of them. Some of my family and friends may want some of it, but if not, it served its purpose by bring me memories, gratitude, and joy. With so many of my belongings now gone, I can truly see what remains and what I appreciate. Downsizing turned from a task into an appreciation and great fulfillment.

Life is simple, I am surrounded by many sparks of joy and no baggage. It feels good to me.

"The power of finding beauty in the humblest things makes home happy and life lovely."
—Louisa May Alcott

"Life truly begins after you have put your house in order."
—Marie Kondo

EPCOT and Koscot

Disney World in Florida has many fabulous theme parks, including EPCOT, which stands for "experimental prototype for communities of tomorrow." The idea, the vision, the plans, and now the amusement park/education flagship has now become known worldwide. My family has been there countless times and we always enjoy seeing what's new. Joe and I took the family there so many times, we became part of large group that had the likeness of our face burned into the granite memory wall. We are etched as #104748.

While many people are familiar with EPCOT, likely none of you know much about KOSCOT. I will tell you more than you might want to know. Glenn Turner was the mastermind of the KOSCOT plan to play off the success of EPCOT (marketing) and developed a multilevel distributorship of selling mink oil cosmetics. Turner was also political and at one time ran for national public office. I was introduced to him through a friend. KOSCOT was one of the first pyramid schemes that many sought to emulate. I fell for it and became a KOSCOT distributor. My crates of mink oil cosmetics arrived in the mail and much to my chagrin, I realized that I had fallen for this scheme. Glenn Turner went on to develop the motivational speakers group called "Dare to Be Great." Again, many followed in his footsteps.

My personal experience was that I didn't want to sell anything. I just loved the product and thought my friends and family would want to know about it. Some did and, fortunately, I sold enough to cover my cost. The bonus was that I had the best product I had ever tried and to this day use mink oil for a variety of purposes. However, I am older and wiser about pyramid schemes. It did take up more than its share of space in my garage and it took years to use it up but thank goodness mink oil is a product that can be used for anything and comes in handy as one matures.

"Sometimes important life lessons are learned the hard (and expensive) way."
—Sharon Cruse

Friends Have an Impact

Joan came into my life at a time that was very busy and chaotic for me. I had a newborn baby, a young toddler, and a slightly older toddler. Being a very young mother was challenging and the roles were definitely very fixed in the 1960s. Men went to work, brought home a paycheck, enjoyed the family in spirts while women were in charge of all things at home. Motherhood was a joy for me, however, and I jumped in with both feet. I always felt, in many ways, that motherhood was a major gift to me. It gave me a chance to parent in the way I wished I had been parented and provided me with great purpose. This was a time when motherhood was considered a sacred job. Yet I was actually still growing up myself and being a mother very young, many things were missed. My house, which was brand new, was usually spotless, right down to the bright, canary yellow appliances in my kitchen. Then I met Joan.

Joan stopped, no matter what was happening, at 4:00 in the afternoon and sat in front of her fireplace if it was cold outside, or on her patio if it was warm, and treated herself to a glass of wine. She relaxed and told funny stories and looked like a doll—even if her house was a mess. She let her kids play, which they were happy to do, because this was "her" time. I didn't know what "her time" meant.

Then my friend Mary invited me over to her house. She, too, left dishes in her sink from time to time, but always made time for me if I stopped over. We loved sipping iced tea on the patio, and we laughed and talked, even leaving a load of laundry in the dryer.

One day, my friend Shirley stopped over. Our children were all about the same age. She had bags of new clothes and bounced around my living room holding up all the items. She was going back to college when her kids went to school in the fall. *Going to college? As a mother?*

These women impacted me deeply. After knowing them a few months, I set some new intentions, I had my first glass of wine, and I decided that laundry didn't have to be kept up. I always welcomed a knock on the door and by fall, I was also picking out clothes and readying for my nine years in college. I finally learned what "me time" meant and I was ready.

"Truly great friends are hard to find, difficult to leave, and impossible to forget."
—Anonymous

The Fog of Grief and Loss

Trying to understand my experience of grief and loss is important to me. Why am I so often in a fog and a stuck space, wandering through so many days? I can't seem to get started, can't focus, and can't explain. It's been three months since I lost my husband, my best friend. During our years of intimate relationship, we often talked about the fact that one of us would most likely die before the other. So, we made many plans to lighten the burden at the time of death so the actual death wouldn't be so harsh and penetrating to the one remaining. We did all the right things, attended classes, made our choices, and had our legal papers in order.

Yet, what I learned is that despite all the preparation done in advance, nothing can adequately prepare us to lose a loved one. Yes, there is grief, but grief is like a container that holds so much more. Many feelings and thoughts flood in at the time of death. Releasing those feelings and thoughts as the days, weeks and months go by is better described as mourning. It the silent tears, the wet tears, and the lying-in-bed staring at the ceiling moments. Grief is eased a bit as we repeat the same stories again, tell everyone what happened, and go through the death again. Each time, more is experienced and mourned. Over time, mourning continues, and grief continues on in a less penetrating way—just a quiet fog. Rabbi Howard Jaffe once said, "You can prepare for death, but you can't grieve in advance." It comes in a powerful way following death. The heavy burden of grief is slowly processed. Much is complicated.

This is a time just for you. No one can do it for you. Those who have grieved before you did it differently, and those who come after you will do it differently. You will do it in your own way. And those who love you best will just let you mourn in your own way. When we mourn and when we grieve, we are forever changed. To know great grief lets you know that you have also known great love.

> **"We bereaved are not alone, we belong to the largest company in the world—the company of those who have known suffering."**
> —Helen Keller

The Gift of Growing Older

Different feelings surface as we grow older. Each age has its own word.

- 16: Anticipate
- 21: Become
- 30: Turn
- 50: Hit
- 65: Achieve

- 70: Reach
- 80: Celebrate
- 90: Appreciate
- 100: Grateful

Watching my husband on this journey, he taught me insight, compassion, kindness, curiosity, and joy. He developed a trademark; it was his smile. As Jay Densie tells us, "Your smile becomes your logo, your business card, how you leave others feeling after an experience with you. It's your trademark".

At each age, there are milestones and touchstones. From a driver's license to being able to vote, to feel mature, to walk in the world, to have made friends, to hold jobs, to get to social security, to qualify for Medicare, to choose a life mate, to become a teammate, to become a founder, to become a parent, to own a dog, to care for something or someone outside oneself—all benchmarks.

We go through passages, from one age to another. It's actually our purpose in life. There is something metaphysical in becoming an adult, a changing adult. No one becomes a sage or elder automatically. One steps into their own story (stories) and become resilient and strong. In our youth, we look for answers and joy outside ourselves. In middle age, we find what we are looking for within community, and by the time we reach older years, joyful and contented people find direction, joy, and health within themselves. It's so exciting and takes such grit, grace and gratitude to go through the years.,

**"Die young as late in
life as possible."**
—Ashley Montagu

Hair: Our Crowning Glory

Several volumes could be written about women's hair. Perhaps little occupies more time in a woman's life. The lucky few pick one style when they are young and, except for a few times in their life, never vary from that style. The majority spend many hours and dollars finding the way to care for their hair.

Some of the lucky ones can do "wash and wear" and let color happen naturally. The majority color, condition, perm, cut, curl, straighten, and dry or blow out their style.

First of all, there is the salon, either where magic happens, or disaster lurks. Salons can be from a lineup of chairs where the shampoo, cut, blow out, perm, color, and other exotic treatments are executed. The artist wields his or her handy scissors, combs, and brushes. This can cost anywhere from the comparable price of a Dairy Queen sundae to a down payment for a car. The process may be the same each week or maybe just from time to time.

One cannot miss the connection between the person receiving a hair service and the one giving the service. The relationship is akin to counselor, confidante, news reporter, family therapist, relationship advisor, and gossip columnist. Depths of trust is built like no other. The hair experience is one that has many facets to it. And then, we can also move on to the manicurist/pedicurist—another whole level of connection if done with the same person each time. Large nail salons have chipped into this industry; however, mini and maxi relationships have been known to develop in this intimate interchange.

There are a million hair salons currently in the United States. they employ 14 million people and generate $44 billion dollars of revenue each year.

**"A good stylist is cheaper than
a good therapist."**
—Anonymous

> **"Hairdressers are a wonderful breed.**
> **You work one on one with another human being**
> **and the object is to make them feel better**
> **with a twinkle in their eye."**
> —Vidal Sassoon

The Real-Life Lessons

My life has been a series of lessons. Some were structured and involved schools, tuition, classes, and workshops. Many lessons were learned from life experience. My Catholic upbringing the first eight years taught me lessons that are with me today. Rituals, beauty, discipline, music, healthy fear, and the ability for deep, personal friendships run through my values and my life. Public high school taught me a work ethic, the value of keeping long-term friendships, the ability to learn from teachers, a sense of community, and especially my business common sense and the ability to speak to any crowd of people. From the Catholic school times, I have also remembered the biblical passages that "where two or three are gathered in my name, I am there." (MATTHEW 18:20)

The school of hard times also has taught me lessons in resiliency, self-confidence, the value of increased discipline, the ability to make choices and live with consequences, the power of beauty, the value of staying current while hanging on to the past at the same time, connection on many levels, and that there is a big difference between the death and the dying process. Through it all, self-respect, love and gratitude, is the stuff that learning comes from.

Everyone seems to want to live at the top of the mountain, but so much happiness and growth occurs while you are climbing the mountain. My higher structured education came later in life, after marriage, divorce, and beginning to raise my three children. At that time, appreciation, hunger and willingness were at an all-time peak. When my therapist asked me, "How do you feel about going on?" the answer was "Ready!" It's been an enchanting experience.

> **"I'm not dismissing the values of higher education—simple saying it often comes at the expense of experience."**
> —Steve Jobs

Take the High Road

We all have experienced hurt, anger, or trauma at one time or another. It's part of being alive. Mine has been often and deep. My major trauma right now is saying good-bye to the physical form of my husband. He continues to live in our apartment through photos, spirit, and felt presence. His wit, his voice, and his actual presence is something I sorely miss and that hurts deeply.

I am not alone in my anguish and loss. A dear friend is facing the pain of losing her only son to an auto accident. Loss isn't always about losing people. Another friend is living through the loss of two of her major senses through an illness, and another feels the sting of making a bad investment and losing a great deal of money—and security—through a really poor decision. Another feels the darkness of a divorce he didn't want, and another heard the news that she will never have a child. For everyone, there was COVID-19 and the lifestyle changes it brought, while others also lost loved ones to the pandemic.

How do we cope and go on with our lives? How do we find purpose, sparks of joy, and relationships that make the world go around?

We choose the high road. This simply means finding what we need to face head on, the assault that comes with suffering loss and grief, and then choosing to go on. This is true for all ages and all stages of life. We hurt, we cry, we share and then comes the necessary need to pick ourselves up, make new choices, adjust, and move on. In this process, we also must face the truth that changes can mean a "new normal" for now and facing that there will be more "new normals" later. Life is always moving. Taking the high road means living fully present and looking for whatever silver linings and strengths that can be found in all major experiences. And then use this stretch of time to stabilize, and be ready to face another trauma, another new normal, a new stabilizing and then the pattern repeats and one *lives* on the high road. It moves from a life of hurt, loss, and grief to a time of adjusting, being present, and connecting with others on the journey of life.

In these connections, we find other pilgrims—not searching for a place but coming home to oneself. It is the story of birth until death and all of the happenings in that span of time. It means to search, to find, to share space, to know the value of a hug, a story, and sense of purpose. It's been said that there are only three things that sum up the purpose and the meaning of life:

- To love one person (or pet and be faithful to that one person or pet).
- To be loved by one person (or pet and be on the receiving end of unconditional love).
- To find and re-find purpose (over and over again).

I've discovered that is a true statement, and that the people, the pet, and the purposes keep changing.

Some else said, "Where there is a breath, there is hope and strength." My story is finding its way and getting a little better each day. I am choosing to take the high road. See you on the journey . . .

**"Weak people want revenge . . .
Strong people forgive . . . Intelligent people ignore."**
—Albert Einstein

Home as Sanctuary

Sanctuary means a safe place where one is protected from danger or difficulty. It offers peace, quiet, refuge, and grace. My home is that for me. It is where I can go through each day taking what is offered me, seeing beauty outside in the green trees and blue sky with a few white, billowy Colorado clouds. I love feeling the air coming through my windows, seeking quiet, and listening to water falling over rocks. I hold a space where life nourishes me. It is good to do whatever one can to make home a sanctuary.

I sleep to the sounds of water, as the breeze comes in three seasons a year and in the winter season, my ice cubes in my water glass do not melt. I sleep especially well when it's cool or cold. The living room holds a big round table where I can share life and laughter. It's so much better than a noisy restaurant. We can actually listen to one another. Cozy spots welcome guests. The guest bed is made and ready for the few who sleep over in my sanctuary. Meditation books are a big part of my life and I love to grab a reading a few times a day.

Bath time remains a spark of joy for me each day. Candles, music, and dark bubbly baths help me shed the stresses and strains of the day and readies me for the floating journey into a quiet and restful night. Each day is a gift. Some days necessarily contain loss, grief, disappointment, and pain. One can't run away from the world. Other days can be foggy days, without clear direction, and many days are filled with gratitude, grace, grit, and plans.

The corner of a room that contains my computer is like a control center. It's where connection with family and friends most often takes place. Welcoming the messages and glimpses into the lives of those I truly love fills my heart, challenges my thinking, and hugs my soul. Writing is my passion and putting words together remains a joy and creative writing releases many daily emotions that surface. Many times, my life has provided me with wonderful homes and land, with yards, flower gardens, and hot tubs; but now my "self" wants a sanctuary and that is how I am choosing to live. It doesn't take much, but it becomes everything.

**"Sanctuary is a place you can feel at peace.
Within you, there is a stillness and a sanctuary to which
you retreat to yourself at any time."**
—Sharon Cruse

Hot and Sour Soup

In the days and weeks surrounding the time of my husband's death, I completely lost my appetite. Several people brought me food, I would try a few bites and then end up saving the rest, reheating, trying a few more bites, and then giving up and throwing it out. One day, someone brought me a carton of hot and sour soup from a local take-out. I found myself eating it and then asking someone to pick up more a week later. Soon, I was buying large cartons. For several weeks, my meals consisted of breakfast, an English muffin with both butter and peanut butter. That was my complete diet seven days a week and for many weeks. Once in a great while, someone would come and eat with me, and I would try whatever they brought. Most of the time, I ate a muffin with peanut butter in the morning and hot and sour soup for lunch and dinner.

I have thought long and hard as to why this was. I've decided it is because peanut butter represents so many things to me. The peanut butter of my youth and how much my children liked peanut butter sandwiches. My husband loved a good peanut butter sandwich and maybe I associate comfort with that particular food.

Then there's the hot and sour soup. During my grieving, what I held onto was my memories of our times together. The word hot means *spice* and *sensation*. As I remember the forty years in love with and spending every available hour with my soulmate, he felt like the spice and fully sensational partner I could have ever known. He turned my seriousness into playfulness. He made me laugh, he brought out all my passion (feelings of every kind—including anger) and somehow, he helped me discover the best and worst about myself—the hot and the sour.

Since the awareness and vocalizing of my needs (comfort and sensation), I have started to add a few more food choices to my palette. Yet, I always know that when I need comfort or awakening, I can have some peanut butter and a bowl of hot and sour soup.

"Sometimes, life seems like hot and sour soup.
It shows heights and valleys, kindness and hypocrisy,—love
and selfishness. What not! The extreme differences."
—Vismayl Karyamsetti

Jars and Choices

Today, we seem to be moving toward a cashless society. We swipe a card or insert a card into a machine and somehow, magically, the purchase is made. Or maybe we press a few keys on the computer. And now, you can even tap your phone near a register and *voila!* How much the buyer of today's goods and services has missed by never handling money, either paper and/or coins.

I still remember the rich treasure of counting out quarters stored in old coffee cans until there were enough cans hidden away to purchase my first automobile, and the satisfaction I got paying for it through my own efforts. The sense of confidence was heady and intoxicating and I knew I could have much of I wanted from life.

Later on, as a young adult, I was able to have glass jars to handle my cash. As my early paychecks were given to me, I put a portion in my savings account, another portion into an investment account (I had liked the idea of investing as long ago as high school), and the rest went into jars. The jars were labeled food, gas, clothes, entertainment, and extra. The choices were made according to the reality of that month. If one came up short, another had to make up for it. At that time, something like illness, not working, or a surprise expense set me "juggling jars." I do not ever remember my family having insurance of any kind.

The work, the planning, the moving cash around, all stayed with me as a young wife and mother. The only thing that changed were sometimes the topics on the jars and the amounts going into them. As one jar became education and more income was coming my way, the years and knowledge began to snowball, I graduated from this frugal lifestyle into another whole life and one that has been good to me financially. However, the principals have taken me a long way. I developed several for-profit companies that each paved the way for the next. The feeling and the relationship to cash at many levels has helped me feel and work through a world today that is controlled by a button or swipe. For me, that never would have been enough.

"For me, the best thing that money can buy is financial freedom to live in the way one chooses."
−Sharon Cruse

Leaving Home at Seventeen with a Dream

Graduating from high school in June 1956 was a big and important event in my life, the first step to adulthood. I cut my hair short, like Audrey Hepburn, whose pixie hairstyle was all the rage of that era. Once I put on that graduation cap and turned the tassel, I was ready for a new life.

I was seventeen and ready to strike out on my own. I had two goals. One was to move to a big city and the other was find a job so I could send money home to my parents. I knew it as I drove the hundred miles to Minneapolis, Minnesota. My hopes to go to college had been dashed by two realities. One was receiving any financial help. It was not possible from my parents because of the disaster of my father's business fire, and two, in those days, scholarships were not readily available for poor small-town girls. Never mind that I had written and delivered original oratories and received number-one state status three years in a row, had worked in my dad's business until the fire shut that business down, had managed to save enough earned money to buy my first car at sixteen the day after I got my driver's license, and that I had ambition. So, I decided to go to work.

I had excelled at typing, took very good shorthand, and was not afraid to speak. Within two weeks in the big city, I had a job at Super Valu Stores corporate office as a private secretary. I worked for Charlie Dugan, Hopkins, Minnesota. He was a lawyer there. I was good at my job, but I fell in love with someone at Super Valu and dating was not allowed. So, I quit my job and immediately applied for one at Red Owl Stores in the same capacity and went to work as a private secretary in the Human Resources Department. I worked there and stayed there for some time until I married the man I fell in love with from Super Valu.

I had learned a very important lesson. I could take care of myself. I never lived at home again after leaving at seventeen. I was on my own. It felt empowering. That lesson has taken me a long distance in life, and I will always be grateful for that lesson. We all find our lessons in our stories.

> **"Leave home with a big, bright dream.**
> **Nurture it into a bigger, brighter reality."**
> —Sharon Cruse

A Lesson in Humility

Whenever I did a major public speaking event, there was a sense of excitement, a combination of fear and hope. I did many over the years, and usually felt I was following plans and had a mission in delivering a message. Some groups were as small as board of directors, some were educational events, some were as big as an auditorium. They all mattered because I knew I had new and different information to deliver and that my audiences were always held in my respect and awe. Never did I feel a hostile or even bored audience,

and I loved being a public speaker. The communication between the audience and myself was wonderful.

I had just arrived in San Francisco for an event. This was to be a large audience and I was both eager and a bit nervous. I was told that 1,000 people had registered so far. That was a larger audience than I had spoken to previously. I knew my material was good. After all, it was original, so they couldn't have heard before anywhere else. I knew they registered ahead of time, so they must want to come. It had been a conscious choice. My years of public speaking had given me a sort of confidence, but one never knows until the end of a workshop or presentation how impactful or useful the information presented will be for this particular workshop. Walking out on stage, taking my place, microphone in hand, I was ready.

When finished, I took a deep breath and smiled as people were on their feet, clapping, and looking happy. It felt like my message was delivered and well-received, which was the goal of the day. I was relieved. It was over and it was worth all the years of living life and developing a message. It sent me on a mission that I had the privilege to get to see come to fruition.

This night, I felt grateful and happy. A thousand people. Imagine! the town I grew up in only had 500 residents.

Later, while looking out the window, I saw a billboard. It said: "Welcome to the San Francisco Arena, where 25,000 will gather to watch and experience Hulk Hogan (the professional wrestler). I felt two things. Humbled and curious. I wonder what his thoughts were like before he walked on stage.

"Nothing in life is permanent!
Be humble!"
—Unknown

Living in Two Worlds

Perhaps one of the most significant things my husband said to me in his dying process was "it's hard to live in two worlds." As a doctor, he knew all about this life and that the body was a machine that had its job to do while one lives on this earth.

He also sensed there was more, and he and I often referred to that part of ourselves as the soul or the essence. As he lay dying, through his actions and words, he shared with me what he was seeing in the rest of the journey, down the road. His words were connecting with Al (his beloved brother who had died several years earlier,) and my husband's word was WOW. He reached out to be helped into the next world. Many people don't talk about such things. My husband and I had talked about the next world many times in our marriage.

As he journeyed more into the amazing process of death, he continued to see more and struggled as he listened to me sing his four favorite songs over and over.

He held tightly to my hand and reached into the other world with his other hand.

He repeated "it's hard living in two worlds." My experience is that there is an art to dying, if it can be allowed to follow its own course. There wasn't much medicine involved—just some pain medications. He did the struggle himself. Three times he uttered the word WOW, and he loved my singing, and holding onto me. One of his final comments was, "Touch has been five-star."

When the people who loved him and also love me told me it was

time to support my husband in his struggle between these two worlds and give him full permission to take the next journey, he let go and simply loosened the grip on my hand. Shortly thereafter, he died with my arms around him.

It was a profound experience, a spiritual experience, and one in which I felt privileged and holy just being a part of the miracle of death. My inside feelings were exploding in every direction, much like I felt at the births of each of my three children. Awe, compassion, searing pain, relief, expectant, grateful, suspended, and many more. It's been said that for a woman, giving birth and letting go of a person are very related. It's like letting a part of you and your essence walk around outside your body and if anything happens to that other person, a part of you goes with that gain or loss. A part of me died with Joe and the rest of me shared in his coming together of two worlds. WOW!

"It's very beautiful over there."
—Final words of Thomas Edison

Making Dreams Come True

As I traveled around the world, telling anyone who would listen that many of my dreams had come true, my statement was followed by two questions from every audience. First, what were your dreams? And second, how did you make them come true?

My dreams were:

- Go to college.
- Have a career that met my values and gave me joy.
- Have a family to love and be loved by.
- Make sense of why I grew up in an addicted family.

- Meet a soulmate to share my dreams and share in theirs as well.
- Stay healthy.
- Have sincere fun.
- Value friendships.
- Believe in something besides myself.

All those dreams have come true!

Some came later, I started college in my thirties and worked hard for every credit. I managed this for nine years while raising my family. When I couldn't find work that was meaningful, I started my own company. Went through a great deal and really wanted each child. I found out that living in an addicted family gave me passion and direction for purpose in life.

About relationships, my plan ended up becoming the kind of person I wanted to have in my life. Lo and behold, when I did just that with all it entailed, he found me. My forty years with Joe were a true dream. When illness hit me almost twenty-five years ago, I needed to change my lifestyle and deal with my own workaholism and have stayed quite healthy since making those decisions. My faith in my own God, universal energy, and something much bigger than me has sustained me though all decisions.

Dreams are simply plans to show us what we want and help us find the paths to get there. People who become helpers to each of us is made up of blood family, families of choice, and closest friends.

TRUST THE PROCESS!

**"Dream with ambition,
lead with conviction."**
—Kamala Harris

Original Oratory

Some are moved by the Grand Canyon, a sky full of stars, a song by Aretha Franklin, and the list goes on. What moves me is great oratory. Martin Luther King, Barack Obama, Winston Churchill, Steve Jobs, Hillary Clinton, Nora Ephron, Gloria Steinem, Mahatma Gandhi, and many more. Oration inspires me and it has been part of my life since I was a young girl.

I do remember speaking my truth often as a child. My father said to me once. "Careful young lady, your sassy talk just might get you into trouble." And it did, and as John Lewis said, "Good trouble." Talking and telling a point of view became my interest, my excitement, and my passion. Debate was important to me because it seemed to me that there was always more than one point of view, and most of the time, all points of view had to be understood in order to make a choice. At first my words came through writing, but by the time high school offered me a chance to write and deliver an oratory, that became my platform.

My uncle, a traveling salesman, would go through my little town every two weeks. From the time I was about eight years old, he would give me a topic. Then he would teach me the principles of oratory and expect an oration on his next visit. Oratory has taken me around the world. When he was an old man, he attended one of my public orations and we both cried . . . but I digress.

My first year of high school, I entered an original oratory contest, and the title was "The Fruit of a Man's Character." It was about honest relationships and how we aspire to them. Not only did it win local and regional contests but ended up first in the state. Next year it was on "Race Relations," again going from local to winning first place in the state. The third year it was about "Personal Responsibility of All Ages," again going all the way to state champion.

I stopped then and didn't pick up oratory again until forming my own company and entering the world of public speaking as a career. For me, it always felt like mission, message, and mentor.

Basically, to me, oratory is simply good storytelling, and stories are what make the world go round and manage to connect us all in important ways.

"Words have a magical power. They bring either the greatest happiness or deepest despair. They can transfer knowledge from teacher to student, words enable the orator to sway the audience and declare its decisions."
—Sigmund Freud

Power and Change from the Top Down

In life, it seems there is always a person or entity that are gate-keepers. They say either yes or no while everyone beneath them waits for a decision. Power very often starts at the top and works its way down—corporations, systems, hierarchies. In the 1970s, this was very evident when I first started working with corporations. Usually, at the top were owners and then boards of directors. At that time of my life, my interest was in helping family systems heal from any number of adversities. My specialty was working with addiction of all kinds: chemical (alcohol and drugs, illegal or prescription, nicotine) and then adding process addictions (food disorders, exercise, and workaholism). While in New York City at a board of directors meeting, I had the chance to meet a board member who was reporting on troubles with production and employee motivation. At the same time, since she knew about my interest in addiction, she asked me if I could help someone in her immediate family. The rest became history as we worked with her family first in helping that family member get through an intervention, and a successful treatment for the whole family, and she had first-hand experience on seeing what a professional difference that made.

We set up a program that included intervening on several families of board members, then department heads, and then employees. This took several months and finally the program was in place in several families and corporations. Eventually, when the next year's board meeting took place, there was a different report on production, finances, and the health of the company. This was the beginning of many early personnel programs, followed by employee assistance programs, and eventually human resource programs.

I stayed on that board for several years in New York and I had the chance to see great change. Some were challenging in the beginning. For instance, "How do you get someone in denial of addiction (whether to alcohol, drug use, smoking, excess eating, excess exercise) who resists looking at the problem and resists any kind of change or help?" Our answer was always, "When it's offered by your employer, when your job depends on it, cooperation becomes much easier. If they refuse, they lose their job and eventually work through more companies until they either take a look or hit bottom. Either way, change happens and the best hope for that person is that change."

In 1976, at Freedom Fest, which I mentioned in an earlier story, we gathered up 26,000 recovering alcoholics in Minnesota alone that had gone through employee assistance programs and whose families were celebrating—sober.

> **"Leadership must be established**
> **from the top down."**
> —Sam Nunn

Powerlessness

Have you ever been so busy you don't how to slow down? It happened to me. I was a young mother, a public speaker, and owner of a very small and struggling company. I was in a workshop and my inner spring wore down. Even though I was sitting in a group of people, I felt alone and the conversation around me simply sounded like humming. I wasn't connecting to anything anyone said, it felt like I was drifting away and in a world of my own. I had finished delivering my lecture and simply stood up, straightened the orange skirt I was wearing, and walked out of the room. I went into a bathroom that was in the locker room of the building, walked into the shower, and stood there screaming—just screaming at the top of my lungs. My world was too big, and I couldn't keep up with the demands. I felt powerless. I don't know how long I screamed. I just felt overwhelmed, and I lost it. When I was exhausted from screaming, nothing changed. I simply surrendered and stopped. I had a new sense of where and how I belonged in this world. When I came out, the workshop was over, and no one was around.

I went home a different person. Why? How? In the moment of feeling overwhelmed and tired, I needed to surrender. I didn't even know what I was feeling. It was some time before I stopped long enough to think and to feel my way through that happening.

Feelings were my clue; thinking was my understanding.

Getting to that moment in my early thirties had been wonderful in some ways and exhausting in others. Living through the alcohol and nicotine addiction both my parents were suffering, finishing high school excelling in my classes and in speech and public oratory, competing in statewide speaking classes, being on my own since seventeen, working in a corporate business world, marrying my husband, entering his world, birth events of three children, taking a leadership role in my church, and the list went on and on. I was tired and overwhelmed.

In a shower stall, in a public locker room, I simply heard me tell myself: No more! From this day forward, my choices will be my choices and they will be intentional. I will choose what I want and accept the consequences. *When I don't have a choice, I will simply accept that some things are bigger than I am, and I will do my best to accept how I respond.*

Later, I found a prayer that says my personal experience better than I could say it myself:

> God grant me the SERENITY to accept
> the things I cannot change.
>
> The COURAGE to change the things I can
>
> And the WISDOM to know the difference.

I live that prayer today. I still wear orange on days I feel my powerlessness and hope for the best.

"Washing one's hands of the conflict between the powerful and the powerless means to side with the powerful, not to be neutral."
—Paulo Freire

Recurring Dream: Finding My Voice

For years. I had the same recurring dream. I called out for help, but it didn't come. I would wake up, trying to breathe. The situation would change but I was always struggling to breathe.

I would be . . .

. . . running in a field, not able to get my breath.

. . . under water and couldn't get my breath.

. . . running away from someone who was chasing me and couldn't get my breath.

. . . in the dark and couldn't get my breath.

. . . in a car and couldn't get my breath.

. . . in a tight, closed space and couldn't get my breath.

. . . in an airplane and couldn't get my breath.

The dream repeated itself month after month and year after year.

Over time, it became the same pattern, and one part changed. I finally saw what was chasing me, always closing in on me when I couldn't breathe and get my breath. It was a notebook-sized sheet of paper with a list on it. All this time, I was slowly getting in touch with my tendency to work too much and keep lists to keep track of what I needed to do.

I began the process of changing my behavior. Instead of making lists, I started using little yellow stickies, writing one thing on each stickie and putting them on my desk, just leaving them there, until I attended to whatever was on that stickie. When I did what I wanted to do, I pulled it off and felt like I accomplished a piece of my "to do's." It was liberating. I also added plenty of time for me and things like self-care.

The visual of being good to myself at the same time feeling a sense of purpose and accomplishment was good. As I clicked off one thing at a time and taking time for self-care, my dreams of being chased by a piece of paper went away. I also began to ask for what I wanted and did so frequently. I found my voice by being more assertive and asking for what I wanted.

I learned that I can change my behavior; It's up to me—no one else.

Self-defeating behavior is both conscious and unconscious. Finding one's own voice and taking time for self is an antidote to recurring uncomfortable dreams.

> **"A woman with a voice is, by definition,
> a strong woman. But the search to find that
> voice can be difficult."**
> —Melinda Gates

Sex Education

Slumber parties were an important part of my growing up. With different configurations of girlfriends, at least once every two weeks I was a part of a slumber party. Four or five girls would get together and spend the night. There was lots of talking, giggling, storytelling, and laughing.

A favorite time was when Joyce hosted. She lived in an upstairs apartment with her parents and younger sister. As we were all between thirteen and sixteen, in a different era, many people did not talk about or teach much about sex. If your parents had not had "the talk" with you about sex, then you often wondered what it was all about and why sometimes it brought out laughter in families. Somehow, babies were born, but kids were often left in the dark about how they came to be. Joyce brought about great interest when she told our group how her parents did sex and that's how babies are born. We listened with rapt attention. We had a hunch since it was a farming community and we all had pets. Hearing the details, however, raised our curiosity.

You might remember the skeleton lock and key. It was a very large hole in the door, and it had a very big key. Joyce's parent had a lock like that between their room and her room. She promised us a lesson we would remember IF we promised to be completely quiet and not get her into trouble. Saturday night would be the night.

We took turns in her room, with the lights off, watching her parents come in, be very affectionate with each other, take their clothes off, and proceed to have sex. It was lovely. They seemed to care for each other so very much. We did that a couple of Saturday nights in a row and felt we now knew the mystery. Remembering Joyce's parents helped a whole lot later in life when sex did become part of each girl's growing up years and, yes, we all had babies.

> **"It's a fine balance,
> listening to people without
> inserting yourself into their reality."**
> —Sharon Cruse

Listening to the Television

In the 1950s, my little town would be able to get television reception as soon as a strong broadcast signal came to our area. My dad was excited about this possibility and rushed out to get that blond wooden TV set. It was a piece of furniture, really, that surrounded the television itself. It was beautiful and had doors on the front so we could close it up when not watching to preserve the inner workings and the precious screen. The television became the prime focus of our living room.

Mind you, our community could not yet receive a strong enough signal to get a TV picture. We knew this, but we were content to have the sound. The first sound we heard was the *Arthur Godfrey and His Friends* variety show. Hearing the Lennon Sisters and Julius La Rosa sing was a great treat. Although we couldn't see, we could listen to musicians, and learn songs that I still hum today. Then we added the comedy *I Love Lucy, The Ed Sullivan Show,* the antics of *The Aldrich Family,* and *The Colgate Comedy Hour.* I think my favorite were the songs on *The Jimmy Durante Show.* Now, remember that we didn't have a picture, only the sound, and that was true, night after night, for a year before the broadcast signal came in. Our screen was simply white snow. Living in Minnesota, I was very familiar with whiteout snowstorms, and this was all we watched as we listened to our shows.

My grandpa was Norwegian and very much resembled Jimmy Durante. For the year we watched snow, I sat beside him on the couch, and he loved Durante's singing and his antics. Grandpa got used to watching snow and enjoyed the music. The night we received a picture for the first time, Grandpa jumped off the couch and asked, "How did I get on the TV? That's me inside of there." I took some time convincing him that he was not the man on the screen.

Nevertheless, we had watched "television snow" for a long time, and it was exciting to have a picture. When you turned the television off, the image on the screen would twirl around and around and disappear into a dot, then flicker off. Watching television was always a family affair, like listening to the radio had been before it. We have come a long way since those days—or have we really?

"When television is good, nothing is better.
When it's bad, nothing is worse."
—Newton N Minou

Timeless Time Plan

At the height of my husband's career, and also my own, we had a hard time finding time for each other. It seemed as though everything demanding jobwise came first, and we took the time that was left over. After too little time together, and fatigue from all our other responsibilities when we got it, we decided we needed to do something different. We created for ourselves the concept of "timeless time." To us, this meant the time we put on our calendar that was just for us. Because our work included weekend work, we had to be very specific. We chose:

One hour a day for each of us—alone, not with each other—and one hour a day together, for our coupleship.

A day a week—just for ourselves—together or alone (we negotiated from week to week).

A weekend a month—just for ourselves or alone (we negotiated from week to week).

At least a week every quarter with each other.

Annually, we promised ourselves a three-week vacation and we took it. Sometimes, we had other opportunities, but we never wavered from our "alone time" and our "together time."

We sat down on New Year's Day and marked all this time in red for the rest of the year on our calendar. We did our best to follow that plan for forty years. Of course, there would be emergencies, change of plans, and some deviation. However, it got much easier to cancel than to plan. We treasured our timeless time.

When one or both of us were invited to something, it also allowed us to say in all honesty, "I already have plans for that time." What gave us peace of mind, organization, and togetherness was a plan that we could follow without a whole lot of conversation or wavering.

Timeless Time is a treat you give yourself, your partner, and your relationship.

"Time has a wonderful way of showing
us what really matters."
—Unknown

Vision Boards

Vision boards mean different things to different people. The two most typical ways to make a vision board are to see what happens while preparing yourself receive a vision or message. The other is to manifest your wants and desires by putting visual representations of them on a vision board. The latter has worked best for me.

Many hours of workshops and retreats had impacted me, and one of those times was the workshop on vision voards. With magazines strewn all over the floor, we were instructed to cut out pictures that resonated with us and glue them to a piece of tagboard, envisioning what our next year would look like. I worked diligently all afternoon and then my masterpiece was done. Our workshop leader was to evaluate ten boards. She had a great deal of feedback for the first few she evaluated and then she came to mine. Her comment was, "Puny effort. You don't have enough imagination or maybe you are just settling in and not wanting enough. I suggest you try again."

I went back to the drawing board and flipped through the magazines again, regluing a new set of images. She liked my revised version. It hung in my office for a while and finally made it to its resting place under my bed. For some reason, I never threw it away.

A few months later, I got a phone call from Phil Donahue, the host of the most popular television talk show at the time, inviting me to be a guest on his show. It was a great surprise and an equally great opportunity. I headed for New York and The Plaza Hotel. It was cold, and I wore my fur coat. A limo picked me up from the airport, and by the time we reached the Plaza, there was a beautiful, gentle snow falling. Getting out of the limo, I had an overwhelming feeling that I had done this before. Yet, this was my first appearance on a national TV show and the first time I had been to The Plaza. Everything was wonderful, and the experience was a special one for me. However, the unshakable feeling of having done this before haunted me until I had a realization. This mirrored my vision board, which was still under my bed. One of the images was a woman, in a fur coat, getting out of a limo with a light snow falling around her. The hotel said, "The Plaza."

I made many vision boards after this and have manifested many other dreams. To this day, I still make vision boards. As I write this, five months into the year, about half my dreams on my vision board have already manifested, and the rest of the year promises to deliver the rest. Needless to say, I believe in vision boards!

"Create a vision board. Pictures of what you want to attract. Every day, look at it and get into the feeling state of already acquiring these wants."
—Rhonda Bryne

Wearing a Bra

Just from my own age, I can safely assume Sister Lucy has gone to heaven. She was a big figure out of my past. She was principal of the Catholic grade school I attended. She was big in size, and she was strict. She was scary to me.

There were lots of other Sisters that I knew who were great role models. Sister Beatrice was old and wise. Sister Peony was pretty and kind. Sister Lucy, however, was like a warden.

One day, when I was in sixth grade, she pulled me out of my desk and said she had to talk to me. I followed her into our small school library, and she started to scold me. She told me it was obvious that I was developing breasts, and someone should have taken me aside and told me about wearing a brassiere (a bra). I was embarrassed and totally mortified. I didn't know what to say. I felt bad, ashamed, and scared.

She told me to go find someone in my family to talk to about it. I went to one of my favorite aunts and told her the story. She took me to a store, and I bought my first bra. I wore it bravely to school the next week and Sister Lucy never talked to me again. I was happy about that, but I didn't stop there. I wrote a letter to the parish priest and told him what had happened. The next year, Sister Lucy was moved to a different school, and I was relieved. This was another case of finding my voice, even at a young age.

Looking back on it now with adult eyes, I know that a kind discussion about this sensitive subject to a young adolescent would have accomplished the same thing. It certainly didn't have to be a scolding.

I kept my eye on the aunt who seemed to know all about bras. She seemed to know many things. She wore jewelry that was pretty. She had hair that was beautiful and different from the norm. To this day, I wear my hair similar to hers. She was kind. Her clothes were always a bit different than the norm. She personified the word "classy" to a very young girl. I kept my eye on her until she died at a classy age of eighty-three. She taught me so many things.

"The right bra can change your world in an instant."
—Laurie Van Brunt

**"And then, there were the sixties, when "not"
wearing a bra became the "in" thing."**
—Sharon Cruse

Twelve-Step Recovery Shortcut

The Twelve Steps of Alcoholics Anonymous are a cultural phenomenon. I won't list them all here, but an online search will quickly find them. They are guidelines for those who have experienced difficulty with any substance or process addiction. Millions of people around the globe know them, live by them, and have had their lives saved because they followed them. They've allowed people who have worked through them to have rich and rewarding relationships and careers, no matter how far they might have fallen because of their addiction.

As Joe and I traveled the globe looking to open us up to different cultures, experiences, and people, along with seeing history come to life. One thing remained a constant: no matter where we went, we found a twelve-step meeting and we learned more there than anywhere. It was our ticket to learning about the world and how people in the world found a twelve-step meeting.

When we returned home, Joe was back in a home twelve-step group.

Whether we were in Ireland, Africa, Scotland or any other country, we could find a twelve-step group. We went to many meetings, were invited to spend Christmas with a family in Norway, introduced to museums in Italy, and met entertainers and singers performing on ships. The twelve-step way of life is how to live well for oneself and for everyone you know and love.

Basically, it's a code of ethics and lifestyle and a good way of life for anyone.

At one point, there was a well-known speaker named Father Martin. He spoke graciously and eloquently about the twelve steps. One night, we were both in a limo on our way to be speakers for a conference. He said to me, "You know, there is a short version of the twelve steps that is a guiding light for many people. Follow this advice and life gets much more meaningful. His shortcut was:

Trust God.

Clean house (your own).

Help people.

When you do these things, life makes sense and things fall into place.

I found that it works for me. The words are easy. The lifestyle changes and responsible choices are more of a challenge, but well worth it

"Life itself is simple—it's just not easy."
—Sharon Cruse

Chapter Seven
Personal Questions

Boredom Versus Solitude

We all feel bored at one time or another—that restless, weary, sameness, repetitive behavior or circumstance that goes on far too long. We end up longing for a change, new scenery, different connections, an adventure. Anything to break up the monotony.

Whether it is the same behavior, the weather, clothes, or even the same conversations with the same people, when we are bored, time drags and time goes on forever. We tend to eat too much, sleep too much, and days drift by without productivity.

Sometimes, there are behaviors that get identified with one person or a group to which we belong. When this happens, as Roger Ebert the film critic once wrote, "a bore or boring group is one that deprives you of solitude without providing you with companionship or meaning." We connect because it means something to us. It adds value to our life. When that value is not there, we feel empty.

On the other hand, when our solitude is meaningful, boredom doesn't seem to creep in. Personally, I rarely get bored, because I love doing so many different things. However, it's easy to recognize when boredom sets in. There is a lack of energy, focus, desire, and joy. When solitude sets in, there just aren't enough hours in a day. It is exciting, the connections are rich, the ideas and production peak. It's up to each of us to know which is our pattern and which is our style. For me, I know. I love being with my thoughts, my ideas, my books, my surroundings, my nest and sanctuary where my home has been made, walking through my neighborhood. The roar of the crowd, discomfort, and conversations of traveling just don't do it for me anymore.

Traveling is something I enjoyed my whole life and now I have done all that needs to be done. My personal intention that anywhere I travel is that it must be as comfortable as I have it at home. My life was as a traveler, not a tourist, but change is now coming. To me, a traveler is willing to absorb the culture, go to new places, discover and take in the adventures that come with it. A tourist wants someone to do the planning and make it easy—not necessarily how it is. Traveling took energy, focus, and stamina. At this time of my life, my needs demand comfort, safety, and ease. I don't feel like a tourist. I just want my comforts to go with me. I have no more need to be pure about traveling. There must be a third word. Comfort traveler, partial tourist, homebody? I know that I am rarely bored, I love solitude, and resist traveling that takes more than it gives. Maybe the word is contented.

"Contentment does not mean that I desire nothing more; it's the simple decision to be happy with what I have."
—Paula Rollo

Cigarettes, Vaping, and Pot

Years ago, looking at classy, sophisticated women, whether in movies, magazines, or in person, usually meant that there was a cigarette hanging out of their mouths and cigarette smoke coming out of their noses.

What that meant is they knew how to covet, crave, purchase, and handle an outside substance. Most of what they sought was relief and some temporary feeling of inner peace. These practices and habits meant feelings could change and one could calm turbulence and loneliness. Most practices and substances cost money and waste precious time, while the industries manufacturing them make a profit from something that is bad for our health in one way or another.

Fortunately, more is known about these practices, and today women have many choices to feel that same relief and inner peace: learning how to meditate, the joy and exhilaration of a walk through the woods, on the beach, or through the neighborhood, finding your special way of moving, swimming, etc.

It becomes a waste of energy, time, and money to put something in one's mouth or nose to get to that place of satisfaction, relaxation, and peace. Finding alternative ways of feeling good are a part of today's culture. Today's woman is stepping out in her own behalf to protect her body, her money, and her well-being. Now, that's classy!

**"Don't take shortcuts through your life
until you know the territory."**
—Sharon Cruse

"I eventually realized I was having a breakdown,
then realized it was a breakthrough, a profound emotional
cleansing, a collapse of the false structures that
I had let rule my life. A breakthrough to a
more genuine state of consciousness."
—Jeff Brown

"Sometimes all a person needs is a hand
to hold and a heart to understand."
—Sharon Cruse

Remembering Those We Lost

Just imagine, in our little quaint Minnesota town Marine on St. Croix there is a celebration like no other that I have experienced.

Memorial Day is just that—memorials. From early morning until late in the evening, the townspeople would gather around Oakland Cemetery to walk through and identify friends and ancestors and bring alive, for a while, all they had meant to those remaining behind. For generations, the stories are told and passed down through interested people. Visitors would bring a thermos of coffee and wander the graves. If the weather was warm enough, they would bring blankets and have picnics on the graves and reconnect with those they loved. The local Veterans Club would bring their trumpets and play taps for any servicemen buried there. Families prayed, and a local band played songs to which all could share and hum along. Cemeteries and the history within them, to me, are like story books. They keep history alive and make the unreal real again. For instance, the grave I saw in Hawaii of a young man killed by a drunk driver and the four beer bottles encased in plexiglass on each corner of the grave, or another of a diploma encased on the grave of the young person who died of illness but had a dream of graduating from college. Or the ninety-year-old with a photo of each of his family he left behind encased in his headstone. Whether it's photos, dates, a saying, they all have meaning. I love the short ones, like ,"Lived Once, Died Once, Loved forever."

My personal history comes alive when I go to the gravesites in Jasper, Minnesota, and say hello to my mom, dad, sister, grandma, grandpa, and many others who lived full lives and contributed to who I am today. A slice of life, nearly forty years, was the life I shared with my soulmate, and even though we spent a great deal of time living in California, Texas, South Dakota, Las Vegas, and Colorado, we spent many important years in this little town called Marine on St. Croix, Minnesota. All of our family shared this little town with us. It was near a major turning point in our relationship, and we decided that we would choose this site to be our "forever place." With that thought in mind, we bought a cemetery plot in Oakland Cemetery in Marine on St. Croix, Minnesota. Graves A and B in Lot 9. Our urn with our ashes reunited again someday will be put in that spot and we shall spend eternity together. Until . . .

> **"As we express our gratitude,**
> **we must never forget that the appreciation**
> **is not to simply utter words,**
> **but to live by them."**
> —John F. Kennedy

Miraval—Tucson, Soul Connection, or Wine?

What is Miraval? It depends on who you ask and their reference. The word comes from two Spanish words and means "view of the valley." It is:

- A wellness and health spa just outside Tucson, Arizona, the spa sits in the desert area.
- Chateau Miraval, a winery in France at one time owned by Brad Pitt and Angelina Jolie that produced a type of rose wine.
- A part experiment, part personal dream that means the symbolic space inside of each of us—our personal landscape.

My personal experience is that it is an oasis of our outside self (the spa in Arizona) and it's also our inner personal landscape. My own experience started when my husband was its first medical director, and it was owned by Bill O'Donnell. I attended many board meetings and had experiences that touched my heart and soul.

Upon inviting several of my women friends to begin meeting with me and completing twenty years of this annual women's gathering, it carved a place in my soul that continues today. While we have not gathered in a while, these women have become family and sisters to me as we connect on Zoom once a month. We have seen each other through the peak moments in life, through sharing intimately, through divorce, through death, through victories, through side-splitting laughter, through the touching of each other's souls. To me, Miraval lives within me and brings me hope and memories, a path into the future, and continued vision. I don't need the external spark anymore. It lives within me.

"Spa days are a necessity, not a luxury. They are the way to a happier, healthier life. Touch, heal and connect. These traits are the ultimate spiritual experience."
—Anonymous

Quality or Time?

Quality or time? It's the age-old question. There are so many answers. How does one choose to have quality of life and enjoy that life? Even the question begs different views. Does one enjoy life if not driving or have the ability to travel? When does someone not have the ability to handle transportation and finances? With the tech society in which we find ourselves diving deeper, some have trouble navigating all the devices—tablets, smart phones, virtual reality. Does life shrink quickly with these culture changes? Keeping up can be stressful and detract from quality of life. Does one enjoy life with family and friends in all parts of the country and globe when past lives were connected and entwined? What is quality of life? Perhaps there is an average cycle of life. It is often believed that if someone has eighty-plus years and moves toward a dying cycle, it's the natural progression of life. Others believe in living way beyond eighty if that is all possible. All we know for sure is that death will happen. Each person, each marriage, and each family need to know their own limits. That comes through talking about it and bringing the question to the table.

The difficulty that individuals and families are sometimes faced with are the heroic means to stay alive. In our culture, we have machines, medications, and measures that can keep the body going beyond the natural cycle. That is true also for younger people who have faced unexpected illness and accidents. There are issues around whether or not to use heroic measures to keep alive, and wills, advance planning, and trusts need to spell out and offer clarity around these questions.

Laws come in and have automatic measures in place unless families request differently. Some people want to hang on, using every possible means, until death can no longer be prevented. This choice is very hard on the caregivers, finances, and the people around that individual. It often bankrupts families. There are statistics that show that too often family members (caregivers) die before the expected patient. Deciding when to accept the natural aging and dying process is a talk for all families to have, to agree on, and to plan for.

My family member wanted the freedom to stay in his own home—even though there may have been more help elsewhere. We had the talk about this several times. "I want to be with you" was his mantra. He was, and he died in my arms. I feel privileged, honored, and complete. Not every family gets that choice. Some choices are dictated by an illness, a disability, or a condition. What is important is that individuals, couples, and families have had "the talk" and everyone feels complete. Grieving loss is one of most difficult tasks one will face in a lifetime.

> **"Sometimes the smallest step**
> **in the right direction ends up being the**
> **biggest step in your life."**
> —Steve Manabelt

Sensitivity: A Burden or a Gift?

I used to hear, "Sharon, you are too sensitive." Basically, I am a serious person. Growing up in a loving, affectionate, boisterous but painful alcoholic family system sets the stage for a firstborn child to become serious—if you are going to make it. There is a lot to do. My parents were often not available (part of the problem is that they were usually having a good time.) It sounded fun, but many times, I woke up in my bed with their guests' coats and jackets piled on top me and I was panting to breathe. My bed was the only place, apparently, to stash their coats and jackets. I learned to sleep as close to the head of the bed as possible so I would be less likely to end up under the pile. That became serious business.

Money was scarce, there was never enough. Early on, I learned the barter system and knew that I better find ways to make money. I pulled mustard out of crops for farmers. I learned to babysit. I worked in my dad's business. I worked in my grandma's restaurant. Was I deprived or was I learning important life lessons?

What was certain is that I became quite serious. It was my seriousness in growing up that led me a pretty exciting time in high school years. I was a good student, I published articles that ended up in the newspaper, my teachers tutored me, I was popular, and I was somewhat fulfilled. I did learn that I could find my own way. I ended up sensitive emotionally, which is both a gift and a burden. I can read feelings in a person or room from ten feet away.

However, the most fun I had was either in my family's boisterous gatherings or in my groups of girlfriends that I trusted 100 percent. I learned to love to plan gatherings that often was with family or my girlfriends where we all loved each other. It's a way I live and value to this day. Too serious? That's debatable. I love my sensitivity. It makes me human and connects me in relationships. In my opinion, there is no such thing as being too sensitive.

But it was Joe Cruse who brought spontaneous fun into my life. That kind of fun was new to me. My fun had always been squeezed in between responsibilities and planned. Joe taught me spontaneity. I will treasure that ability forever. He made me laugh and play with abandon.

"You deserve to be loved by someone who looks at you like you're the only one in the room ."
—Jason Robinson

Seriousness Versus Joy

Seriousness came to me much easier than a smile. In one photo taken when I was a small child, as I sat cross-legged and staring into the camera, my mother captioned, "You will be president of something someday." And, of course, I was many times over. Middle school and high school clubs, oratory debates, turning in a 14,000-word booklet entitled "The Problems of the American Negro." I was fifteen years old.

Don't get me wrong. I laughed my way through high school with my girlfriends and certain family members, but my default was always "seriousness." Imagine my delight when meeting my husband who was a spontaneous and delightful character. He made me laugh. Sitting in the car under the moonlight with happy and romantic music on, I was reading him my list of marriage requirements I had for this "later on" marriage.

Of course, he was serious as well or he wouldn't have ended as a physician, a surgeon, on political committees, and an officer of every club he ever joined. But it was the first time I had known someone who had a quip or a one-liner for every situation that could make people laugh, who smiled every day of his life, and winked at himself in the mirror in the morning while shaving. He experienced plenty of downtimes, but he went through them, savoring what could be learned, added it to his life experience, sincerely felt gratitude to go on, and lived that lifestyle. It was the most attractive trait I had ever seen in another person, and I knew I wanted to spend the rest of my life right beside him. My life felt complete with him in it.

He made me smile, he made me laugh, and everything became more fun for me. Perhaps I hadn't noticed that feeling like the responsible person most of my life had brought much heaviness. Once together with Joe, people would observe my laughter, my sense of humor, and find me pretty delightful to be with.

Those traits were challenged when recently, I was in a group and were assigned to "tell a joke or funny incident" from our personal lives. I was very surprised to recognize that was a very difficult task for me and I couldn't do it. My personal awareness and knowledge is that our history stays with us.

> **"It stands to reason that anyone who learns to live well will die well. The skills are the same—being present in the moment, and humble, and brave, and keeping a sense of humor."**
> —Victoria Moran

Storytelling: Boring or Skilled?

True storytelling comes from within and is enhanced by life experience. To truly attract the attention of others, the story needs to have an element of the human condition that we all share. Little Red Riding Hood had a grandma. The Three Bears had to learn to use their voice and express their differences. *Schindler's List* tells the story of the Holocaust, struggles and pain.

On a smaller scale, we tell stories of birth, death, life, relationships, and purpose. There is also the input of color, comparison, timelines, and the passage of time. A meaningful story is the one that is told and the one that listens. All of us have stories, some of us tell them, and some dismiss storytelling. I remember a family member telling me "You tell too many stories and sometimes you embellish them." My response was, "So?" Both are skills. One comes from knowing one's topic through experience. No one knows it in the same way as the storyteller. If something has been remembered, it has a good chance of being valuable to the storyteller. To put together a story is a skill in itself. To have the talent to add color, time, and texture to a story (whether it's the exact way the experience happened or not) is a second skill.

If someone is listening carefully to the story, it's the sign that it's a good story. Whether it's exact or filled out with texture is immaterial. What is important is the telling and the listening. May you find the storytelling part of yourself. Examine your childhood, your teen years, young adult years. Then, as you grow older, tell the stories of each decade. There will be people in each decade that will relate to you, and you will have become a storyteller. In the end, stories are the thread that tie us all together. Some become books, some become movies, some bind communities together; stories are the energy that feed friendships, movements, protests, and families. Become a storyteller, an enraptured listener, and keep the storytelling artistry alive.

Be proud to tell a story and then another and another and finally share with your family and friends that you are proud to be a storyteller. As time marches on, stories are what we have to share. This kind of sharing opens a window to our soul. Have the courage to tell your story. If someone else shared that experience, their story might be a bit different. Yours belongs to you! Keep them short and to the point. Details are your richness to savor.

Your stories will outlast each of us and have an energy of their own. Do not underestimate the value of a story. All of history is a story. Treat it with respect.

"Stores are a slice of "your life." They are a gift of yourself. They invite others into how you lived and do life."
—Sharon Cruse

Whoever Really Knows Real Estate?

Winters in South Dakota and Minnesota can leave one craving warm sunshine and vacations to Disney World. We drove around and came to a beautiful tennis resort near Haines City, Florida. We fell in love with the beauty, the grounds, the restaurants, and the setting. Upon returning from that trip, we were now the owners of two condos. One for us and one for our visiting guests. For several years, we wintered at Grenelefe Tennis Resort. Joe loved following the PGA standard golf that went on there and he himself played on a nearby course.

We bought season passes to Disney World and every day made the half-hour trip to Main Street and walked the Magic Kingdom streets for our morning walk. The second condo was used primarily by family and friends for their trips to Florida during the winter months. Many memories were made there. By the late 1980s our grandchildren were getting busier in their own lives and our work kept Joe and I traveling a great deal. We talked some of trying to sell both condos as they had served their purpose. We knew that selling winter condos was sometimes a difficult issue, but at least we owned both and they weren't timeshares.

By chance, one morning at the beauty salon, which was always a source of the latest news, I heard a rumor that someone was in the area looking for condos. As a matter of fact, they were looking for many condos as they wanted control of the homeowners' association. I immediately called the owners of the association and, sure enough, it was true. A Japanese company called Sports Shinko was in the area buying up condos. They

would offer 25 percent above market value and pay all closing costs.
The offer was good until 5:00 PM that day. By 4:30, we had sold both
condos, made a profit, went out to dinner, and arranged for our furniture to be shipped to Rapid City, South Dakota. By the weekend,
the Florida experience ended.

I couldn't have planned it any better, and all because I happened to
go to the beauty salon at just the right time. One never really knows.
Life can and does unfold in mysterious ways!

**"Look at market fluctuations as your friend
rather than your enemy. Profit from folly rather
than participate in it."**
—Warren Buffett

Chapter Eight
Relationships

Let's Do Both!

Joe and I had long careers that, while rewarding, were also demanding. It involved lots of travel, running through terminals at hundreds of airports, short nights of sleep, and then coming home to carry on in our training/treatment programs. We often worked twelve-hour days, seven days a week. Needless to say, we were tired.

One day, my husband announced he wanted to retire. It was after delivering almost 4,000 babies, doing countless surgeries, building two teen drug-treatment programs, starting the Awareness Hour (now attended by many thousands) in Palm Springs, and culminating with the founding of the Betty Ford Center in California. After all this, he was definitely ready.

We decided that we would take a major trip. To us, that meant maybe a month long or so, and we would choose somewhere we both wanted to visit. Trying to decide the destination became a source of conflict. It was our first major argument. When would we take this trip? I was eight years younger than he was and not quite ready to retire, but I did consent to go on a retirement trip with him. I went back to work for a few more years. When it came to where would we take this trip, the argument picked up again. Joe wanted to go to Hawaii, or England/Wales, or Greece. I wanted to go to Italy, or Easter Island, or Toronto (to see theater), or Egypt. The argument started on May 1, 2000. It continued over the summer with no resolution. We were at a turning point. It was the beginning of a new century. We both wanted a trip but to different places.

In October 2000, a brochure came in the mail. We had done many cruises and were on many lists. This one was from the Princess Cruise Line on the Royal Princess, and it was an "Around the World in 100 Days" cruise, so around three months. It included nearly all the places on both of our lists: Hawaii, England, Greece, Italy, and Easter Island, but it didn't include Toronto. It had this strange place called Kusadasi, Turkey. We were both enchanted with visiting Ephesus in Turkey.

We looked at each other and said, "Let's do it!" We'd both have all the sites we wanted to see. We had our health, we could work out the time, and we both follow both our dreams.

That was the beginning of the plan from that point on that, when possible and each of us wanted something meaningful, we would try to find a way "to do both" and that remained with us all our days going forward. We set sail in January 2001 and had a trip that went straight to both our souls and remained there the rest of our lives. We went around the world and found new worlds in our individual selves and with each other. The "do both" philosophy goes a long way.

**"It is our choices that matter in the end.
They shape our life at all stages."**
—Sharon Cruse

**"It is choices, Harry, that show what we truly are,
far more than our abilities."**
—JK Rowling, Harry Potter

Big Sisters

Fresh out of high school and in my first job, I was looking for a way to contribute something to the world. Leaving my sister a hundred miles away back home was challenging emotionally for me, so I decided to join the Big Sisters program. What that meant was to give time once a week to empower, educate, and encourage another younger female. They assigned me with a young lady named Henrietta Schurer with whom I met once a week. She was thirteen and I was only nineteen, but I took the responsibility of learning how to mentor seriously. The city was new to me, so we explored together. We visited museums, talked about books, went on picnics, and planned for what she wanted in her life. Henrietta had not eaten in many restaurants, so we had hamburgers together in a restaurant. I had a car, so we drove in the country and walked around lakes.

Sharing my passion for photos and scrapbooks, I took photos of her, and she started her own albums. The excitement of taking pictures and going back to the drug store the next week to pick them up was one of her favorite new learnings. My second passion was writing, and we would write short stories and share them as well. Over time, we both learned and grew from this experience. She moved on to high school, and I grew into other mentorships. But this was my first and the memories are still with me.

Sometimes, I am surprised that I remember her name and the activities that we did. Important stages in our own learning perhaps stay with us forever. To this day, mentoring another woman younger than myself gives me purpose, meaning and joy. Over the years, it has been exciting to watch women grow into their own voice, their own histories, and their own passions. Sisterhood is one of the great joys of my lifetime.

I wish I knew where she was today and how she remembers the same time.

"Volunteers do not necessarily have the time—they just "take the time". You make your life by giving parts of your life."
—Sharon Cruse

"Volunteers are not paid because they are worthless, it's because they are priceless."
—Anonymous

Foreign Exchange Students Win Hearts

Little did we know the adventures we were in for when we decided to take in foreign exchange students. Over the years, we had Ann, from Finland; Irene, from Germany; Bjorn, from Sweden; Marc, from France; and Yoko, from Japan. By this time, my children were in high school and active in their own lives. However, we had one boy, so our first goal was to provide Pat with brothers, and he found them in Marc and Bjorn. Then when Pat and my older daughter were preparing to go off to college, we chose Ann and Yoko as fellow girls in our family. All but one came for fourteen months at a time, and one program was shorter. However, what a delightful path we went down with this decision. We learned new customs, food preferences, and how far advanced schools were in other countries schools compared to ours. After being in the United States for a year, the students were required to go home and repeat that year. That was surprising and a bit disconcerting .

While the students came to learn about life in a different country, we gained so much from them:

Ann was delightful and so creative and talented. She taught us so much about Finland and its grace, its creation, and its gentle nature.

Bjorn taught us that modesty was different in Sweden. He had all brothers and was used to walking around nude in the family. We had girls and different customs. The first time he walked into our living room nude, we were shocked. A few heart-to-heart talks addressed all of our needs, and we loved our time with Bjorn.

Marc suggested that Pat come to France and when he was in college. Pat took him up on this offer and he spent time in France with Marc's family. It was wonderful for him, and we were so happy to know that Marc opened doors for our family.

After only three weeks with us Irene, became ill and was diagnosed with Type 1 diabetes. We assumed her parents wanted her to come home. She really wanted to stay, and her parents eventually agreed, so we all learned how to be on a team and to be there for someone with this serious disease. Her parents trusted us to care for her, and she flourished at our home.

Yoko had many different customs to teach us. Even after I ran over her foot with my car—she was not hurt—her family agreed that she was happiest at our house, and we carried on.

Life gives us these opportunities and we knew how to take them. When one looks, one finds.

"Being an exchange student is letting your heart be divided into several small pieces and taken to distant places in the world and hope we will meet again."
—Former foreign exchange student

Foster Children Steal Hearts and Love

When my children were growing up, it felt very important to let them know about as many facets of life as possible. Since they were raised in a home that valued children, I felt we could afford to share what they had with someone else less fortunate, so we signed up to be a "foster family." We had a few different young people who stayed a week or two and then we were introduced to Keith.

At the time, Patrick was eight or nine, Sandy was seven and Debbie was five. Keith was four. The story unfolded. We all had so much fun and now we had two boys in the family and two girls. The days, weeks, and months went on and Keith became so important to all of us. We could barely remember when he wasn't part of our family. He joined us on camping trips, we made chocolate chip cookies together, we played games together, and always had meals together with the whole family.

Four years passed and we felt as though foster care would go on forever. Then one day, came the call we didn't expect. Keith's mother wanted him back. It didn't seem possible that they would come get Keith and we could never see him again, but that's the way the foster system worked at that time. It may still, I don't know. How does one prepare for this kind of grief and loss? Four years is a long time, especially for a child, and this was half his life. Disbelief was followed by anger, then sadness. Keith cried every day. It was huge for Keith, who had become part of our family. We had tried to adopt him, but that was not part of the original agreement when we agreed to give him care. It was very painful for all of us, but I had no choice.

Somehow, I knew we had to find a way to make this as comfortable for Keith as possible. That took some doing from each of my children, but we all got behind that plan. First, we went on a shopping trip. We tried to make it sound like a natural happening and fun. We went to the store and bought him a sailor suit, complete with a hat for the trip. He found that a bit fun. Then, we prepared boxes to go, with treasures to open for the first early days. Next, we told stories for him to remember. Sometimes, even today, I wonder about how much of that he remembers. Then the day we all dreaded came. The kids all said good-bye first and then a sitter took them to a park. Keith and I sat on the front steps, sailor suit and all. When the foster care reps came, he took their hand and looked at me and said, "See you later, Mom." I think they walked him to their waiting car. I was watching, but my vision was blurred by all the tears. Then the car was disappeared from view. It was a lesson in grief and loss for us all.

Fast forward years later. One of my daughters was in junior high, and she told me she saw Keith, who was now in the seventh grade at her school. He was fine, he seemed happy, and he was delighted to see her. They talked and somehow both knew—it was another time and place—but Keith still lives in all of our hearts. We won't forget that name and all the lessons that came from being a foster family.

**"You might be only temporarily in their lives,
they might be temporarily in yours, but there is nothing
temporary about the love that is shared."**
—Tonia Christle

Love Collision

Joe Cruse was fifty when we met, and I was forty-two. It was clearly another chance for both of us. My mother always said, "It's so good you didn't not meet one day earlier." Our meeting was not random, and it was not a simple "Hello, how do you do?" It was a forceful collision. We needed every moment we had lived to that moment, spent in effort, struggle, loss, joy, grief, work, appreciation, and spirituality. It was all preparation to take on the task of coupleship. Both of us had loved before, but the earth hadn't moved yet.

Earlier relationships had been part of what everyone and our culture demanded of two people. We had both married before and we had loved and reared our children the best we knew how. We were both actually children having children before we knew much about adult life. We had both also experienced the single life and were quite happy with the careers, family roles, and adventures we had carved out for our individual selves.

Then in 1982, the earth did shake and move. Joe entered my world first, as he tells the story. I was on stage, speaking at a conference, and he was brought up to the stage and we were introduced. He met me and that was how it remained for a few months. Then I was hired to help select staff for The Betty Ford Treatment Center, and he was doing the hiring. I met this quiet, gentle, humorous, confident man and very soon afterward, our Hawaii date happened (also told in this book). By the third date, I had job interview questions ready for this man when he asked me to marry him. He had his own bottom-line questions. We interviewed, we continued to collide, and we went forth into a forty-year marriage that was the greatest coupleship either of us ever imagined. My mom added to her comments about us years later, saying, "It was so good you found each other. No one else could ever have lived up to either of your expectations. You were a perfect match."

"Have enough courage to trust love one more time and always one more time. Sometimes two people fall apart to realize how much they need to fall back together. Love alone can rekindle life. A successful marriage requires falling in love many times, always with the same person."
—Maya Angelo

Snoopy, Pat, and the Red Mustang Go to College

We were always a "dog family." While some people adore their cats, horses, birds, gerbils, or other animals as pets, dogs were our thing.

My life started out with Blackie, and then along came Scottie, Skeeter, and Pudgie. They were all special and had their endearing habits and talents. Pudgie, for instance, could sit on her hind legs and hold an ice cream cone with her two front paws. Skeeter slept in a tiny cake pan. Long before having my own children, I was a "dog mom."

When my son, Pat, was born, my grandmother gave him his first dog, Blackie. We graduated to many more, including Scottie (again), Pepper, and Snoopy. We don't have oil portraits in our family, but we do have an oil of Snoopy and Pepper and the important roles they played in our family. We all learned to care for a living creature outside ourselves. They were all special, but Snoopy and Pat were like bread and butter. She was all love and had beautiful black fur and sparkling eyes that lit up every time Pat came home from school in the afternoon, or got down on the floor to wrestle with her.

Then life transitioned, Pat grew up, and was accepted to the University of Colorado at Boulder (CU), far from our home in Minnesota. When it was time for him to leave home, Snoopy, the princess, made it clear that she was going to college as well. She watched every move Pat made as he packed up and it was finally clear that Snoopy was moving to Colorado with him. He wouldn't even consider leaving her behind while he took the much easier way to get to Boulder—flying and shipping his belongings. Dogs aren't allowed in the dorms, so we bought a condo so that Snoopy could stay with Pat. When it was time to go, we loaded up in the car, an old red Mustang, with all of Pat's stuff and, of course, with Snoopy.

We were not riding in comfort. We had to navigate across several states in that loaded-down car. The trip could not be made in one day, so halfway to our destination we spent the night in a motel. We needed to rest after driving all day, but no one got much rest. Pat sat by the window all night watching the car to make sure no one took his life's possessions. Snoopy, who had become carsick during the day, threw up on the motel's orange shag carpeting. I tried my best to sleep since I had another long day of driving ahead of me. We eventually made it to Colorado safely and set Pat and Snoopy up in their new home. I gave up the car and flew home.

Snoopy and Pat thrived at CU. She helped him through the transition to living away from home, and he took seriously the lessons he had learned about being a responsible pet owner. They tooled around town in the red Mustang like the three musketeers.

Snoopy and the red convertible remained constant but while at CU, Pat accepted a foreign exchange student assignment in France. Obviously, Snoopy came back to live with me while he was overseas. The red car waited in the parking lot in Colorado. When Pat returned back to CU three months later, so did Snoopy.

The months passed and it was time for Pat to graduate. The red Mustang was getting old and could not make another Colorado to Minnesota trip. At that time, there were no buyback programs and nowhere to store a car with problems, yet the vehicle could certainly withstand a few local miles. Pat and Snoopy left the car in the school open parking lot, with the keys in it, and assumed someone would simply take it, use it, and abandon it somewhere. That was okay with us. Yet, upon returning to the parking lot three months later, the Mustang was still there—keys and all! We eventually found a way to dispose of the car permanently.

Snoopy went on to spend some of her post-college days with Pat and died of natural causes. It was a peaceful death. We were all enriched by her presence in our lives, as we hope ours were to her.

"People love dogs. You can never go wrong adding a dog to the story.
—Jim Butcher

"We cannot cure the world of sorrows, but we can choose to live in joy."
—Joseph Campbell

My Daughters as Mentors

When my youngest daughter, Debbie, told me she was going to home school her five children in Alaska, all my fears came to the surface. They lived too far away, they wouldn't have the socialization of classmates, it would be too hard to keep track of five children at different ages all having different needs, and on and on. She herself had a traditional education, undergraduate and graduate accomplishments, and she was determined she was qualified to homeschool them. I was somewhat relieved that her own education had been in higher education, and I trusted her. Then I experienced the way she taught: letting them choose their own interests; encouraging them in every step; letting them learn from the consequences of their mistakes and, generally, learning from life. When I asked her how she was going to keep up with all the latest learning techniques, she said, "I don't plan to. My role is teaching them to love to learn and they will find their own mentors and teachers." I watch in astonishment as they learned to do just that. Some found tutors (on their own), some learned from the computer, some took internships and read all the time. Some played sports for the local public school sports team. They all found their way. They all have meaningful careers, (airlines, engineering, Disney World, and one is still in college). They love their careers and are well-traveled. I learned from my daughter and know that homeschooling is very important to many people.

When my middle daughter, Sandy, was fifteen and in high school, she and her sister helped me put together my first company, a publications company. She used her skills and her bubbling personality to come up with the idea that by changing both girls' voices, they could represent several departments in the company: ordering, sales, public relations, bookkeeping and marketing. She was quite the entrepreneur. Our little company took off and became quite successful. She always knew she could do it and developed the sales and marketing approach the company enjoyed. It was so surprise to me that she was both kind and smart. Her early volunteer approach (Candy Stripers, baby-sitting, etc.) led her to increased confidence in sales and marketing. It was no surprise for me to see her car with a large artificial donut installed on top as she ventured into the sales world by selling donuts. Later life found her being a registered nurse, a psychologist, a Reiki therapist, and a spiritual healer.

In trying to be a good mom, I always believed my girls would become my mentors and they both have done just that.

> **"Mentors are those who allow you to see the hope inside yourself."**
> —Oprah Winfrey

It Only Takes One Teacher

I was the luckiest student in the world to have two life-sharing teachers in high school.

Mrs. Mett was a stickler for English and speech classes. I already had been spotted by my Uncle Vern (from the city), who was a salesman and spoke so eloquently compared with the farmers in my Minnesota small-town community. He commanded attention and told me, "I can teach you to talk. Want to learn?" I did! As he traveled through our county, he would stop by my home and give me a lesson. This started as early as when I was in second grade. One week, he would assign me a topic (ketchup, boats, bed, knife) He asked me to study and find out as much as I could about that word. Then next time he came through town, he wanted me to give him a one-minute speech about that topic.

I told Mrs. Mett about that task, and she said she would help me. She would take me aside at recess or in study hall and coach me. Over my high school years, my Uncle Vern's coaching moved from my needing to give him a one-minute report on a word, eventually to one hour and the task went from a word to a subject. Mrs. Mett kept up her efforts for my four years of high school as I excelled in speech and communication skills.

By my senior year of high school, I had written a 14,000-word essay on "Negro Issues in the USA" and came in first place three years in a row in the state of Minnesota "Original Oratory" category and joined the debate team.

Later in life I became a trainer/educator and public speaker and spoke in conferences all over the USA, Europe, Mexico, and Canada. Mrs. Mett and I stayed in contact until she died at ninety-two.

Mr. Holos was my business administration teacher four years in high school. I love the idea of business systems and learned so much from this man. I learned about income, outgo, savings, bonds, passive income, staffing, marketing, startup costs, and insurance. I learned to make flow charts, budgets, supervision, etc.

When I graduated and went on in life. I put all this knowledge to work in my personal life and tried to follow the principles of good business.

By the time I was sixteen and could drive a car, I had worked and bought my first secondhand car and paid for it by myself. I also had money in a savings bank account and kept spending cash in a metal bandage box.

By the time I was in my forties, I had founded a small company that grew and became an internationally known business—and it's still going strong. I am grateful every day for two caring small-town teachers. Mrs. Mett wrote to me just before she died and said that "working with my passion and courage" was the greatest experience of her career and she thanked me for our time together.

**"The influence of one good teacher
can never be erased."**
—Unknown

Pepper Goes Home Again

It was so hard to watch our dog Pepper continue from simply growing older to debilitating aging. Her role as family dog was firmly established and she was our everlasting princess. Her big brown eyes met mine many times during the day.

Dog lovers recognize the clues of aging. Little appetite, slower gait, sleeping more. We, the guardians, look the other way as long as we can, pretending to ourselves that everything is okay. There is plenty of time, we hope. We find ourselves giving more time and attention, petting longer, smiling a bit more often. It's a game we play with ourselves, and it works for a while. Yet, in our heart, we know.

On a big brown braided rug, Pepper lay sleeping many afternoons, and then the day came when it was just too difficult for her to stand up. She was of a size that was a challenge, but we started carrying her outside to go to the bathroom. Then we would carry her in and settle her onto the rug in the way she liked, with just a streak of light coming in from the sun outside. She would lazily spend the next few hours until she needed to be carried out again.

With my husband at work, and my children at school, it became my responsibility to take Pepper in and out. After a long talk with my vet, one day I carried her to the car. Setting her in her place on the front seat beside me, she watched, and I looked down. We both had longing and some strangeness when our eyes met. As I handed her over to the vet, I petted her, and our eyes locked that one last time. It was a long ride home, an empty pillow and an imprint that has never left my heart.

Pepper, the princess, went to a new home; one where she can run and play again.

"If there are no dogs in Heaven, then when I die, I want to go where they went."
—Will Rogers

"Dogs come into our lives to teach us about love. They depart to teach us about loss. A new dog never replaces an old dog. It merely expands the heart. If you have loved many dogs, your heart is very big."
—Erica Jong

Chapter Nine
Surprises

The Colorado Blizzard of 1982

The year 1982 was an important one to me. My daughters and I had been in Colorado visiting my aunt and uncle and also there specially to celebrate my son's graduation from college. Colorado has a reputation for rapidly changing weather. As they sometimes say, "If you don't like the weather, don't worry, wait five minutes and it will change." This is no exaggeration. It can be sunny and warm in the morning and snowing in the evening.

As hardy Minnesotans, however, snow didn't frighten us. The weather today, however, was different. When we woke up in the morning to a snowstorm, ready to fly home, the first clue should have been that our taxi did not want to pick us up for the ride to the airport. We called my uncle who also said no, he wouldn't take his car out, but we were welcome to stay as many days as we needed to. Ever the workaholic in those days, I didn't want the extra vacation and my daughters were eager to get back to their friends. We tried another taxi company and they said, "Be right out." It was a harrowing trip to the airport, and almost zero visibility with snow falling faster and heavier than I had ever seen before.

We got to the airport and the real adventure began. Needless to say, all flights were canceled, and we were assigned a gate to wait until the storm passed and flights resumed. It was an experience like one I'd never had and have not had since. The first few hours were like all airplane delays: crowds, long lines at the bathrooms, and constant noise and complaining. The first day was uncomfortable, and this morphed into a long night. By morning, it was turning into a surreal nightmare. The airport ran out of water bottles and there was no water in the drinking fountains. The bathrooms were out of toilet paper. Crying babies were everywhere. And the snow was still coming down. There was a run for food from the vending machines. There was no coffee. The crowd was building, and everyone was anxious. One of my daughters became ill. The luggage department was going through the crowd bringing back our checked baggage. The baggage rooms were being converted into emergency rooms for stranded passengers. We had four bags which were full to the brim now with Christmas presents. We made a small fort out of our bags and put them around the two seats we still had. One daughter had given her seat to someone elderly. As we approached our second night in the airport, panic was setting in. We were tired, hungry, and so sorry we had not stayed in Westminster with my family. We survived the second night, and they began to call for flights for when the airport re-opened. That, too, was tense and traumatic.

Three days after we were dropped off by our Jeep taxi, we boarded our plane to fly home. We have never forgotten the Denver airport and the Colorado blizzard of 1982.

"Experience if the hardest kind of teacher.
It gives you the test first and lesson afterward."
—Oscar Wilde

Carl and His Love in the Philippines

Long before Joe and I left on our world cruise, we were with our personal healing program in the Black Hills of South Dakota. One of our guests was a guy named "Carl." He loved the program, and his favorite activity was hiking in the mountains behind our center. He was in our program facing his cigarette addiction and also recovering from a divorce and adjusting to a new love in his life (his fiancée). He was close to completion of his stay with us when, one early morning, he went for a hike with his group. On the hike, Carl suddenly fell to the ground and died of a heart attack. We were all devastated and worked with his parents to complete all arrangements. The group attested to his joy and satisfaction and near completion with our program.

Fast forward, close to ten years later. Our ship, the Royal Princess, was sailing around the world and we were in the middle of the ocean just having left Easter Island. I was attending a yoga class and went forward to thank the teacher and tell her how much I enjoyed the two weeks in her class. She asked me where I was from. I enthusiastically told her South Dakota (I always loved being from there). She asked where in South Dakota and I mentioned Rapid City. Her next comment stunned me. She said, "My fiancé died there just about ten years ago, and I have never had closure." She went on to tell me the story of how she was not welcomed into the family by Carl's family, and they didn't include her in any of the memorials or service for Carl.

Needless to say, I was flabbergasted at this coincidence. I told her of our connection to Carl. I wanted to help her find the closure she needed and deserved. So, together, we went to the ship's captain and asked for a phone line to South Dakota. We were successful in connecting with the leader of Carl's group in South Dakota. He assured her that Carl was very happy in South Dakota—the happiest he'd been in a long time. He had worked hard in the group setting and had found new healing. They had gone walking together, and Carl had remarked how much joy and peace he had found in the programs and that he felt contentment. She was then able to find her own

She found the sharing and connection she so needed in order to grieve Carl's death. Life unfolds and the universe is to be trusted. Thousands of miles disappeared, and humanity found a way to connect and heal.

"An invisible thread connects those who are destined to meet. Regardless of time, place, and circumstances. The thread may stretch or tangle, but it will never break."
—Ancient Chinese proverb

Intruders

Living in Las Vegas was like being on vacation in an adult playland. It was part fantasy and very much real. We lived there just a little over twenty years. While we enjoyed the best of entertainment, from the Rat Pack to Siegfried and Roy, often it was the free lounge shows that knocked your socks off. The food was amazing, and, at the time, it was plentiful and inexpensive.

We hosted our children and grandchildren countless times. Our guest bedroom was full more than empty. Yet it wasn't the entertainment and shows that brought us the most joy. Pure joy came from joining each other and tap dancing our hearts away, being a part of a loving group that supported each other in the early retirement years. The three golf courses in our neighborhood were my husband's first love, and he golfed every week when he could squeeze it in between his computer club, chorale singing, and a men's group that discussed the meaning of life and what was happening in the political and business worlds. We were as busy in our years in Vegas as we were in our hard-working younger days "at work" in our professional lives.

However, there was a chink that evolved. Our house was on a quiet rock-covered lot on the golf course. Because I can only sleep with open windows, I started hearing intruders, usually around 2:00 AM, people walking around on the rocks outside. It unnerved and frightened me. I usually waited it out but every night it was the same . After about two weeks of these nightly noises, I called the police. They found nothing. The pattern evolved. I heard nightly intrusions of someone walking on our rocks. It stopped when I would get up and call the police.

Imagine my embarrassment and surprise when I had my annual doctor's visit during this time and found out I had a pretty serious case of tinnitus and the sound of "ringing in the ears" mimics exactly someone walking in the rocks. It was hard explaining to the police what was happening, and as I worked to rid myself of tinnitus, magically, the "intruders" went away forever. Finding out that laying on one's ear can trigger an episode and getting up stops it was both a relief and an embarrassment.

> "Tinnitus—having to learn to live with it is a constant
> struggle. Always keep hoping— do not give up."
> —CDB

John Kennedy

One day, the phone rang at our home in Las Vegas. We received very few calls there as they were typically filtered through our office. We always had unlisted and unpublished phone numbers, so we knew it was either someone we wanted to hear from or someone who had connections to get our phone numbers. This caller, however, didn't fit into either of these categories. He said he was calling for John Kennedy's office, "Not the late American president, he was quick to point out, but John Kennedy, president of the Intercontinental Hotel in Maui. He went on to say that he wanted to thank me for saving his life through one of my books. As a way of showing his gratitude, he offered Joe and me the luxury suite on the top of the hotel for a two-week stay. All expenses would be complimentary, including all restaurants in the hotel.

I thanked him back and stood a bit bewildered. When I grasped what he was saying, I assured him I could not take a gift like that. I wrote books for the general public, and it would feel unethical to accept such a generous gift. I declined, thanked him again, and left the conversation.

After I hung up, I started explaining to Joe what had just happened when the phone rang a second time. The caller said it was the office calling again and vouchers had been put in the mail, even though I had not given him an address. Nevertheless, he assured me that Mr. Kennedy would leave the suite open during that time, and if we changed our mind, it was ours. The vouchers arrived and Joe and I talked it over. We felt that it would be wasted if we didn't go. We made alternative housing plans and left for Hawaii on short notice. Joe and I always felt it was wise sometimes to just "go for it." We were greeted at the airport with leis, which were changed out each day and left outside our door. We had so many different kinds. The suite was magnificent. We enjoyed the delicious hotel meals and had one of the best two-week vacations ever. We were never able to meet John/ Jack Kennedy. Both names were used. This was all anonymous and many times we wondered if his name was really John/Jack Kennedy.

**"Nothing in life is ever simply random.
Everything that happens is supposed to happen.
Trust the Process."**
−Sharon Cruse

Dinner Out or Hawaii?

It started out with a consultation. I was working as a systems therapist in Austin, Texas, and Joe was the medical director of The Betty Ford Center, which was in Palm Springs, California. They were hiring staff and requested my advice about how to build team spirit. It was a good meeting and ended up with a dinner at a nearby restaurant. I knew of Joe, and he knew of me, but we had not worked together before. As dinner wound down, he asked if I would like to have dinner again two weeks later on a Friday night. "On second thought," he said, "How about two dinners? I can't make up my mind which restaurant I want to take you to. Save Saturday night as well." I thought this sounded a bit strange, but it was plausible, and so I said yes.

The two weeks passed, and he said he would pick me up early to look over the plans for his project and then we would go to dinner. As

I got into his car, he explained that the first dinner would be in Hono-
lulu at Ruth's Chris Steak House, and we had just enough time to get
to the airport. Was I game? Certainly I was game! He then explained
that the rest would unfold. Joe was in California, and I flew in from
Austin, Texas. I had no luggage or changes of clothes, but Joe bought
me all that I needed for the trip on the spot.

He booked us separate bedrooms in a luxury hotel and a tour of
the islands. He had been a doctor at Trippler Air Force Base and at
Trippler Hospital. He wanted to show me his former life in Hawaii.

Our second dinner would be two days later on another flight coming home. Was I game? He handed me a bag with toiletries and a gift
card for anything else I needed for the weekend.

Feeling cherished, loved, and excited, I headed off to Hawaii for
my first real date with this exciting, full of adventure man who turned
out to be a scientist, a doctor, a gentle soul, and a barrel of fun. How
could I be so lucky? Little did I know, I was headed for a forty-year
adventure. He never disappointed.

**"Grow old with me,
the best is yet to be."**
—Robert Browning

Red Rose

During a professional trip to Texas, my hiring sponsor bought
me a pair of red down boots. It started a lifelong passion for boots.
I also accepted a job from them to move to Texas and in a job that
paid me more than double of what I was making in Minnesota. More
important than the salary, the job was going to give me a chance to
help me follow my passion of trying to bring help to children growing up in addictive families. On a cold Minnesota day, I bundled up

in my red boots, heavy clothes, red mittens, and a red stocking cap and headed to Texas. With children who needed money for college, I welcomed the pay boost, and it was my intention to accept this win/win situation.

It's a long drive alone on the highway from Minneapolis, Minnesota, to Austin, Texas. It was snowy and windy but, thankfully, the highway is straight. Along the way, when I grew exhausted, I would stop at roadside restaurants, rest, pump gas, and start another part of the trip. Sometimes, I would slide, but I always had complete control of the car. As I moved further south, fortunately, the weather got better.

One day, at a restaurant, a truck driver came up to tell me "We are happy that you made it this far. Don't know how far you are going, but we just want to wish you well." I was surprised by this encounter and asked how he knew I was on an extended trip. He replied ,"Well, we've given you a handle. You are the Red Rose and we have kept track of you on our walkie-talkies since you left Minnesota. We just wanted to be on hand, should you have a problem." Surprised, I thanked him and got back into my car, just a little surer of divine protection. I also treasured my red boots. I wore them until they were shreds.

**"Truckers say good-bye to their family to
supply the needs of yours."**
—Unknown

How Romantic Was That?

My serious nature and workaholism helped me design workshops that started on a given Friday night and continue for a week ending on a Sunday afternoon. It was a way of stretching a one-week workshop into a ten-day event. It worked for those attending, though not so much for those conducting. The workshop was in Austin, Texas, and my role was directing it. Fatigue started to set in at the end of the workshop, and I looked forward to some rest and relaxation.

One of the participants was my good friend Joe Cruse who was very interested in learning more about my work. The end of each workshop was near, and we all formed a circle to share what the experience was like for them.

Listening intently, it seemed as though the workshop had been meaningful to those attending as we went around the room and people shared their learnings and insight. My adult daughter was in the audience, and I was eager to hear her feedback. Joe Cruse was in the audience and his feedback was important to me as well.

My daughter gave very insightful comments and it seemed she enjoyed my work very much. It meant a great deal to a mom. People continued to share and when it came to Joe Cruse, his feedback was very surprising. He commented that he learned a lot. Part of what he learned was that "Life is short, we are all responsible for our choices, and we should know what we want and ask for it." He then went on to say, "Sharon, will you marry me? Your work is important, but so is your well-being, and I want to be part of both. Will you marry me and make me the happiest guy on earth, and I will do my very best to take care of you."

Needless to say, I was speechless. Yet, I found my voice and said, "Yes, I will marry you." Then, as a faithful workaholic, I continued on with the ending and closure of the workshop. Everyone hugs at the end of the workshops. When they were all finished, you can imagine that Joe and I had a very special hug!

**"When I look into my heart, I see only you.
If you look into your heart, and only see me, then we
should spend the rest of our lives together."**
—Anonymous

Soybeans and South Dakota

When you live in Las Vegas, you meet the most interesting people. Joe and I heard some of the most wonderful and amazing stories. There was plenty of glitz and glamour to be shared as people moved to our area to find privacy, fun, outstanding restaurants, and some of the best live music in the world.

In our neighborhood, we met a very fun couple. Our interest grew when we asked them where else they were living. Most of our neighbors lived somewhere else in the summer and came to Las Vegas for the winter season. We were happy and surprised that they also had a home in South Dakota. After becoming friends, we planned to see them the next summer as we headed for our home in the Black Hills. They had told us they were farmers, and we were welcome to spend a night on the farm with them. They gave us general directions.

Coming from a small farming town in Minnesota, I knew about farms, cattle, chickens, pigs, and crops. As we drove into the town of Pierre, South Dakota, I stopped at a grocery store to ask for directions. I told them I was looking for the (name deleted) farm and they replied, "You are standing on that farm right now. There are thousands of acres to that farm." I asked for more complete directions or where I might find the house and they directed me there. We followed and came upon thousands of acres of soybeans, and nearby was the house. We were on one of the largest soybean farms in the country. That was our friends' (name deleted) farm, and they were out working in the yard, growing a summer veggie garden. They showed us the machinery shed where they kept equipment. Just two or three of their many machines would cost more than our entire home in Las Vegas. I learned how soybeans were grown, where they were shipped, and what an industry it is. I was fascinated, and we both enjoyed our overnight at "the farm."

"If you ate today, thank a farmer."
—Unknown

Chapter Ten
Spirituality

Angel Room

In our home in the Black Hills of South Dakota, we had a room called "The Angel Room."

Over the many years of doing counseling, teaching, and training, our dear friends and staff lived with us while attending many of our programs. Many gave us gifts of angels and we collected angel treasures, statues, paintings, books, etc. The room was full of white wicker furniture, many green plants, and nearly 300 or so angels of some kind. Joe eventually wrote a song called "People Are Angels" and many people who experienced The Angel Room still remember that song. It begs the question, "Are angels really people, or are people angels?"

This room also housed a table that held yellow stickies. On them were the names of the many people we prayed for. The house had many bedrooms, and our staff loved rotating through our home while working in our training and/or treatment programs. Early in the morning, we would gather in the room and pray for our day's work in the programs. The room also had picture windows and a large twelve- person hot tub. When the day's work was done, we would all gather in the hot tub for our staff meetings. It was a glorious way to build friendship, trust, and team spirit. This type of gathering went on for many years, and today those friendships still thrive.

After finishing a program, Joe and I would continue the practice until the next staff would arrive and another program would begin. The Angel Room was the hardest room to leave when we sold our precious home in the beautiful Black Hills. At that time, I packed up my precious angels and, little by little, I have given away all but thirty-five, which still live with me today. I know and love each one and each evokes a memory and carries a particular energy. I still wonder, "Are people really angels or are angels the people we know from day to day? Mmmmm . . .

"Be kind to strangers because it's the loving thing to do. You never know, they could be angels."
—Scott Curran

"I could not have made it this far had there not been angels along the way."
—Della Reese

Blessings, Sages, and Wisdom

Stories and memories are what make each day rich and full. Finding the people who will walk this journey with us is like looking for the pot of gold at the end of the rainbow. Upon them, I shower my prayers and my gratitude.

Blessed are those who know how to make me feel I am the "me" I remember. Fun, energetic, young, with a gigantic sense of humor and always "ready to go."

Blessed are those the ride in the car with me. They travel back roads and accept that busy highways and intersections are too hard for me.

Blessed are those who know I choose safe battery candles and understand that I still need a few with fragrances.

Blessed are whose who pull out their credit cards and treat me.

Blessed are those who speak low and calm, and do not take over conversations.

Blessed are those who ask questions and then listen for answers.

Blessed are those who master the art of slowing down. As we age and deal with life's health issues, they show patience and walk with us and wait for us and show respect and care.

Blessed are those that know at a deep level that they, too, will age. That is why knowing, acting, and loving is so important. We will all be there someday. Everything that is worthwhile and freely given shall be received someday.

Blessed are those who cook for us and remember how much we like homemade food: casseroles, comfort food, and peanut butter sandwiches.

> **"Elders and sages often take longer to focus
> and concentrate, but when we do speak,
> we have a lifetime of wisdom."**
> —Sharon Cruse

> **"Aging is not lost youth, but a new stage of
> opportunity and strength."**
> —Betty Friedan

> **"I may not be learning a whole lot right now,
> but I am using what I know."**
> —Sharon Cruse

Catholics and Publics

Coming from a small farming town in southern Minnesota influenced my formation of concepts. In the town of only about 546 people (the population sign just outside of town often changed when people moved in and out). We had one Catholic church and six small Lutheran churches. The Catholic church was the largest. We had one big Catholic school and one big public school. As a child, I put all of these institutions in one basket and believed there were only two religious denominations: Catholics and "publics" and I believed that there was a strict separation.

Imagine how hard it was to live that way. I didn't walk on public sidewalks, use public bathrooms, drink from public water fountains, or play in public parks. I didn't share this with anyone else. I just assumed that was the right way to do things. Did some of my Catholic friends do some of these things? Yes, I just thought they were breaking the rules and would have to deal with their own consequences.

I was in third grade when I began to really pay attention to my lifestyle compared with my friends. There were many things that were different with my "public" friends, but I thought that came along with money and privilege, as well as religious preference. Sometime, somehow, over that third-grade year, I learned that it was okay for me to use public buildings and privilege. I could be both public and Catholic.

Catholic school was more than a school. It was a way of life, a framing of existence, a wonderful experience of belonging and installation of a deep faith.

It also was confining, exclusive and a hierarchy that didn't last a lifetime for me. More to come in other stories.

"Autobiographies and memoirs are only to be trusted if they reveal something disgraceful."
—George Orwell

"If you grow up in a very strong religion like Catholicism, you certainly cultivate in yourself a certain taste for the intensity of ideas."
—Brian Eno

Changes Happen Fast in Church

Those who remember very traditional parishes or spiritual congregations will relate to this story. In the 1960s and 70s, I was part of a traditional church community: it included a building devoted to worship and a regular Sunday service. I was raised Catholic, and my children were less so, but each attended Catholic School for a while. We knew the routines and the Sunday services. However, this was a tumultuous time in our country: the Vietnam war was raging with protests against it and the civil and women's rights movements were in full swing. I was in college, and all of this helped fuel me to become an activist. Priests and nuns were exiting, and church services started being offered in halls, auditoriums, town halls, and the like. The walls in our home were covered with fabric messages to "get involved in human and social issues," and the banners in our house said, "Bloom Where You Are Planted; Friends Are the Flowers off Life" and "Put Your Time, Money, and Energy Where Your Values Are."

The Catholic church changed their worship altars from the congregation facing the priest's back to instead turning them around and inviting the people to come in. Instead of the wafer hosts we had taken for years, we brought homemade bread to church and shared our wares on Sunday morning. Instead of meeting in a traditional church, we met in a school auditorium.

Children growing up at this time were dazed by the constant change in their families. We settled on a church called St. Joan of Arc, with Father Egan. No personal relationship. It was an exciting, uplifting, challenging, time. My children grew up with excitement, chaos, and living with people who spoke up about what they believed. Values and lifestyles were formed. I treasure those days and hope my children do as well.

My children were used to me asking them to lie on the floor, feet in a circle, listen to the vibes of the group, and find your mission. We would do so to the sounds of Ommmm . . .Yes, I was always influenced by the signs of the times, but some things never changed.

- Family was important and always invited along.
- I was willing to go where they lived as well (even if it meant chocolate chip baking at 2:00 AM in our house).
- Friends were always welcome in our home and invited in

- Respect for all was a necessary part of our lives.
- We cared for each other, our friends, and each other's wishes and goals.
- We did not believe in a hierarchy.
- We took time out for fun, such as my letting my children's teachers know they needed regular mental health days. Those were days we played.
- Animals were treated with respect, love, and care
- History and connection mattered.

"It was not a perfect time, perfect parenting, perfect anything. But it was a very good time and a journey we all took together. No regrets."
—Sharon Cruse

The Life-Changing Cursillo

There are many paths to the core of God. One that Christians often take is participation in The Cursillo. The three- to four-day weekend was started In Spain and at the time I was involved, it was focused on Christianity. At this point of my life, I am interested in all the paths that lead to whatever each person believes in their own life. I support Christianity, Judaism, Buddhism, and Kindness. My life would be much emptier if I didn't believe in anything beyond myself. I have faith and I have walked many walks.

Here are the lessons that have stayed with me a lifetime from my Cursillo days:

I learned PERSONAL FAITH as I listened to the stories of those sharing from their life history.

An important part of my life is sending and receiving letters, e-mails, gifts, and connections with my friends. (In Cursillo, these tangible forms of energy are called Palanca.) My apartment is full of Palanca.

Lasting TOOL OF TIME, MONEY and ENERGY. Learning to make decisions around my values continues to happen by reflecting on, "Where do I spend my time, money and energy?" I live according to my values, and when I am making choices in every area of my life, I ask myself, "Where do I spend my time, my money, and my energy?" It works both ways. I make decisions around my values, and I understand my values based on my behaviors. Naming both my values and my behaviors has helped me all my adult life.

Skill of making COMMUNITY. Many things connect the souls of people. I think my favorite is "sharing stories." Community can be built around a cup of coffee, a glass of wine, while walking, sitting in a favorite spot, workshop, or audience of 1,000 people. I have done each of those. I respect and treasure all my communities.

Camino means "have a good walk." Each walk becomes a pilgrimage where the connection with one's soul is often touched. The value of WALKING has been incorporated into my life for many years. Walking is reflective, healthy, and incorporated into my life. Many have walked the Camino Santiago. However, the essence can be in every walk you take. It's more a state of mind one can visit as much as it is a place. My camino is Hecla Lake, Louisville, Colorado. The message I like to share when I meet someone is "have a good walk."

**"We get together because of similarities,
but we grow with differences."**
—Unknown

God Hole

There is often an inner emptiness that occurs in our culture. It could be that there is a spiritual void that is occurring for so many. I am not referring to religious attitudes, but rather a "life spirit" that propels us to welcome and enjoy each day. With the experience of excessive isolation, excessive "trauma drama news" and a sense of loneliness, we often seek meaning and balance.

The kind of spirituality that I am referring to is the energy that brings us hope and excitement, and which provides meaning in our life and death. Just how do we increase intellect, deal with our changing bodies, or search for health and mental growth? Sometimes we are tempted to just keep busy or have just enough energy to look forward to or follow all the traditions we know and attempt to do everything we "should" do. Then we ponder, "Will my life be happy and fulfilled?" Surely, it will have more meaning."

What many come to realize is that, once recognized, perhaps learning about the spirit is as simple and as difficult as coming to know ourselves. Many spiritual mentors have preceded us and paved the way: Christ, Gandhi, Dag Hammarskjöld, Buddha, Ram Dass, and scores of other spiritual leaders have a burning interest in love and justice. They showed compassion in their lives and inspired others by their trust and unwavering faith. But all the sermons and stewardship and self-sacrifice become meaningless gestures and hollow noises if we do not have love and understanding for each other. This love has its origin in our relationships and pervades all our relationships.

Our power comes from within. It is not from an outside source. Personal meditation allows us to become attuned to our inner strengths instead of looking for answer to "life out there." As we come to know and accept ourselves, more and more of our inner spirit is released. We are free to figure out our own meaning of life and free people help set others free. We fill our God Hole.

"If outside validation is your only source of nourishment, you will hunger for the rest of your life."
—Unknown

"Life is not primarily a quest for pleasure, as Freud believed, or a quest for power, as Alfred Adler taught, but a quest for meaning."
—Victor Frankl

God Winks

My husband Joe used to look in the mirror every morning and wink at himself and say, "Hey, you did good!" Starting every day like that meant that he came to breakfast with a smile, a sense of gratitude, and ready to take the best from every day. It was his habit, and I came to especially love that part of him. It would rub off on me. As I approach my days now, I try to do the same. Some mornings, I just don't feel like it, but when I do try it, it works.

Belonging to one or another of the twelve-step programs, at different stages of our lives, both Joe and I had many opportunities to decide to make every day be the best day we could possibly have. Many have called it "a coincidence" when two things collide in a powerful and unknown way. Joe simply called them God messages. He then read the powerful book *When God Winks* by SQuire Rushnell and found the word *Godwinks*. That word became part of his language and sharing for the rest of his life.

Now it's part of mine. It's my privilege to watch for them, to see them, to remind others of them and pass along the concept. It's perfect, and it makes so much sense of so many mysterious happenings. The concept gives order to a sometime chaotic world, gives us reason to hope and make connections in the events of our lives. It appears that there is more going on than we can see, touch, and feel. It brings comfort.

I am a dreamer, a creative person who has faith in the goodness of people and learning to recognize and incorporate Godwinks into understanding my life, my choices, and my actions has given me great insight, wisdom, and gratitude for my own life. Try it! You have a treat ahead. Watch for the coincidences and serendipity in your own life. Once you undertake a long, hard look into your career and choices, you will discover that Godwinks happen more often than you thought.

**"Coincidence is God's way of
remaining anonymous."**
−Albert Einstein

**"Every coincidence becomes an
opportunity for you to become the person
the universe intended you to be."**
−Deepak Chopra

Hollow Reeds and Energy

As a young child growing up in a loving but distracted family, I spent a great deal of time alone. Somehow, my knowing always told me there was some kind of universal energy, sometimes called *God*, sometimes called *spiritual energy*, and I always knew the universe was looking out for me. Somewhere, in those years, the lesson of "leave room for the spirit to get in" was not lost on me. Always, it felt important to take care of my "land rover" as Joe referred to our body.

It was my job to take care of my body, my heart, and my soul. This energy would take care of the rest.

My life did my best to find fuel for my body. Spending time, energy, and money to take the best care of it that was possible at any given time, trying to fill my mind and thoughts with contemplative prayer and meditation, choosing the people in my life that would support these thoughts, and tried to "leave time and space for the spirit to come in." The idea of hollow reeds became my mantra.

My attraction came forth when, as a child, I loved to eat green dandelions. The flat green leaves are like leaf lettuce and my family made a dish of dandelions, hot boiled potatoes, hard boiled eggs and bacon/vinegar gravy that I crave to this day. Spring meant the yellow dandelions, and I always found them beautiful. I really looked forward to blowing the seed pods away when they turned to drying out. Dandelions became a hollow reed. Clarinet became the instrument of choice for high school. I love art with hollow centers. Many different cultures find ways to create "hollow reed concepts." We find that hollowness in art, in vases, in instruments, and in tradition.

In my meditations, the goal is to picture myself as a hollow reed, open to what this spiritual energy or God is trying to tell me, and it is the way I choose to start my day. Hollow areas are how that spirit gets in and becomes a guide. Truly, none of us can do it alone—we need that energy.

"There is a crack in everything.
That's how the light gets in."
—Leonard Cohen

Rituals and Growing Up Catholic

Bear with me non-Catholics. That is the word I grew up with. No mention of Buddhism, Judaism, Hinduism, or other types of Christianity. As a child, my reality was Catholics and non- Catholics. It was the way of small-town living and education for me. Trust me, my education and learning opened new worlds for me along the way.

Today, it's wonderful for me to celebrate my past and treasure my memories. Being a different person today, I honor and respect some rituals and traditions while many have gone by the wayside.

It was a great adventure to adopt "pagan babies." Much of my time was working hard to get pennies and nickels to put in my metal Band-Aid box until I had enough to turn them in and buy a pagan baby somewhere in the world and on the map. It would be someone who was not lucky enough to be Catholic and American. The intention was good and later life took me to many of the countries that I truly believed that my pennies and nickels were supporting babies in those lands. To this day, politics, missions, and the plight of people remain a constant source of interest and concern for me, and it all started with trying to make life better for "pagan babies" in early grade school.

Many hours of my early life were spent in praying the Rosary. Rosaries are beads and a type of meditative practice that was practiced in early times, very Catholic, and continues to this day. I own special rosaries. Prayers are connected to them and said over and over in a meditative fashion. Learning to practice the meditative practice of saying the Rosary or attending a session where all are saying the Rosary together is a peaceful happening. If I ever have a sleepless night, I can pull one out and start the practice and soon I am sound asleep.

I didn't like confession, but I did it regularly for many years. Confession is good for the soul and gives a way of "living life." It's like making amends that is part of the twelve-step tradition. Saying "I am sorry" is perhaps the best tool for relationships. I have said it many times, and each time, it cleansed my soul. As a child, we would go into a little booth and the hearing person would open a little door and we would confess our sins of the week: venial (little sins) and mortal (the serious ones). It taught me that saying "I am sorry" has cemented many relationships.

**"Rituals are the formulas
by which harmony is restored."**
—Terry Tempest Williams

Chapter Eleven
Traditions

Apple Dishes

In my family, they are known as "Anne's Apple Dishes." The world has a bigger story. The dishes, a pattern called Franciscan Apple, were crafted in California in 1940, and today are eighty years old. Their production story is long and interesting, and they are still reproduced by the Wedgwood Company. The apple pattern was used by television to set the stage for another era and were used exclusively by the shows *The Golden Girls*, *I Love Lucy*, and *The Big Bang Theory*. Air Force One uses Franciscan Apple dishes, and they can be seen on the shelves of Elvis Presley's Graceland. Its lesser-known sibling, the Desert Rose, was used in television's *Northern Exposure*.

The dishes became important to my family in the 1950s. My mother and father started collecting them by the piece. My mother didn't really own anything of value. They came to mean "love" in my family. Each piece was a gift from my father or some family member. Only adults could wash and dry them, and they were brought out each Sunday after church for a special meal. Over time, mother accumulated an eight-piece serving set, along with some supporting pieces, and they became family treasures. Everyone loved coming for a meal and using Anne's dishes. The year 1961 was tumultuous. My dad died suddenly at forty-six years of age. Being a businessman in a small town, the community poured out their love and support. However, the loss of an earlier fire, coupled with my father's early death, took its financial toll, and mother lost her house in 1962.

The only thing she was able to take as she moved into my uncle's extra rooms, were the Franciscan Apple dishes. The dishes survived the death of my father, the loss of the house, and a move 100 miles away.

The dishes were too much for my uncle's apartment, so mother· stored the boxed dishes in a friend's basement. My mother went to work at a drive-in restaurant and the dishes remained in storage. One night, the apartment burned down, and my mother lost everything again. The dishes, stored at a friend's, survived. Later, we brought the dishes to my mom's home where my she spent her last days. We used them again for a few years. During this time, she called my sister and I to her home and told us that when she died, she would divide the dishes in half so we could keep the tradition going. She would give the cookie jar to my brother. That was fine with us. After she died, my sister Sue gave the cookie jar to my brother, gave me Mom's Timex watch and a couple of other items, and my sister decided to keep all the Apple dishes. For years, I felt hurt and figured Sue had some reason and let it go. I started my own collection, piece by piece. When my sister died way too young, I figured she would right the earlier wrong. I was stunned when she gave them all to one of my daughters. The old hurt returned. However, within a couple of months, my daughter, knowing about the hurt and not having the same history with the dishes, arranged to have the whole collection brought to me.

It is clear to me that the Apple dishes carry a spiritual history. They have survived time, loss, fire, storage, family pain, and transport. I believe they carry a spiritual and karmic energy. They get used. By now, hundreds of people have shared in their beauty. Sometimes, I gift a few pieces and it is my hope that someday they will end up in the hands and hearts of my children and grandchildren. They have lived in many places and have now found a home in Colorado. They have seen tragedy, joy, togetherness, separation, and bring their own energy. A legend of "Anne's Dishes" has been created. The are a karmic link.

**"Our most treasured family heirlooms
are our sweet family memories. The past is then
never dead. It is not even past."**
—William Faulkner

Trips of a Lifetime in a GMC Van

We were riding through our little summer community in Minnesota after a visit with all seven grandchildren. We had taken turns stuffing them in the front and back seats of our sedan. We taught the kids to squish together and showed them how to "double-buckle" in their seats so we could get all seven of them to fit. Two to a buckle in the back seat and one on my lap meant we had all seven in the car. If we took a mom along for our adventure, we had to squish even more. On our way home after one of these adventures, we saw a big white GMC van with a "For Sale" sign in the back window. We followed that van four miles and then down a long driveway. When they stopped, we stopped, and made the deal right then and there. Later that night, I drove the car home and Joe drove the GMC (which became known simply as "the van"). It was better than we imagined as the back two seats folded down into a queen size bed and had a small television screen installed for the back seats. We were now ready for real adventure, and it never disappointed.

No more double-buckling for us. Everyone had a seat belt and could grow up safely. We put hundreds of miles on that van, in Minnesota, Las Vegas, Rapid City, trips to Disneyland, Legoland, farms, dude ranches, etc. Sometimes, a mom went along, and many times it was just Joe and me and seven grandkids. That van saw ice cream stops and pizza stops. If kids got too tired, we could stop and put down the back seat and they all could take a nap. It was well-stocked with movies, cartoons, and entertainment.

On Memorial Day and the 4th of July, when our little town boasted parades, bands and crowds that line the streets to be part of the Marine Celebration, we could take "the van" downtown early in the morning, filled with snacks, hats, horns, and flags. We could park the van with the back facing the parade. Later in the morning, we would walk downtown and all pile into the van storage and have a place in the street saved for us. The van became the central system for food, chairs, and our place during the holidays.

Owning a van requires special work and expense. When in the Marine house, surrounded by trees and land, the van could sit in the driveway. When we loaded it up to take our necessary items back to Las Vegas in the fall, the van could not sit in a Las Vegas driveway because it was against the association rules, so we had to find a storage lot and buy a space. Then the van was winterized and put away for six months. It would feel like something was missing until about April or May when we headed back to Minnesota for the summer. We definitely had two lives: Las Vegas glitter and glam and Minnesota with the deer and "the van" and countless visits by grandchildren. We never gave a thought to expense, work, safety, vulnerability and liability. The van was our eighth grandchild.

"Life is a beautiful ride."
–Sharon Cruse

"You don't have to be rich to travel well."
–Eugene Fodor

Dreams Do Come True

Some days, a writer just wants to reflect on the gratitude of growing up in a small town in Minnesota. The wonder and the mystery of my life remains deep and plentiful. My growing up years were the days before traffic, before virtual anything, and when there was time to ponder how many stars there are at night or lying on a blanket and making up stories about cloud formations. There was time and a sense of wonderment about so many things.

I loved the radio shows, homemade food and the time to eat it, talking and sharing every meal with someone who was already sitting down at the same table. Don't get me wrong, things were not always happy or perfect. In my family of origin, we dealt with smoking (yet no one knew yet how devastating that would come to be) and there were the times of too much alcohol consumption (although in my growing up days, the addiction hadn't progressed to a serious level).

We were also short on money and security. However, there was still bliss that lasted and took me through the hard times when addiction and circumstances did take their toll.

The mere fact that I was able to grow up and fulfill my first dream, getting married, having three perfect children, have a brand-new home, and keep my friends and family was fulfilling. Later, my dream of going to college and becoming a professional therapist was very confidence-building for me, and the idea of writing a book became a dream that morphed into twenty-three published books and several movies. Little did I know that, as a single mother, I would meet my soulmate and the man one dreams about. Years later, the dreams kept coming, life kept unfolding and it brought me so much more than early dreams. The forty years of my soulmate and enjoying family, our coupleship, and walking through the world together was a major happening.

Some mixture of my faith, my willingness to work hard, the quality of life I find in family and friend connections, the good fortune I had to be born into the family I learned from in my early years, and my gratitude does reinforce my belief that life is what it is and it's our job to bloom where we are planted. A small-town girl finds total contentment at this time of her life.

**"I'm just a small-town girl
with big-city dreams."**
—Unknown

**"If you can dream it,
you can do it."**
—Walt Disney

Spaghetti and Turkey: Full of Feeling

In our treatment program in the Black Hills, group leaders (doctors, psychiatrists, psychologists, and various other helping professionals) would fly into Rapid City and our company would offer a series of eight-day treatment and educational programs to bring hope and help to the participants in these programs. They would be housed in our home (a beautiful log home named Crestwood), nestled in the beauty in the hills. Staff meetings were at our living quarters (in the angel room and the hot tub) and the treatment programs and participants in our programs were at our center about fifteen miles away.

Janice was an amazing woman who worked for us making sure we created a family feeling in our professional lives, and then that "professional family" went on to become the staff that worked with healing other families and individuals. It was an amazing setting and plan. We also had an office staff and building in Rapid City that did all the arranging of all this housing and operation, and our treatment center was another site nestled into a cozy setting just south of Mount Rushmore, on the other side of town. Programs went on year-round with a business staff of ten people and a group leader network of sixty of the best therapists in the nation who flew in for our programs. Our programs had a set of cooks who prepared three meals a day for the forty participants in each program.

If you're wondering about turkey . . . the programs repeated every couple of weeks, and when the group leaders arrived on a Sunday night and settled in, Janice would cook a turkey dinner with all the fixings for the first night of every program —just to make everyone feel like they were coming home. I ate a lot of turkey, dressing, mashed potatoes, and gravy during those years. It was like family every time a new staff was ready to start a new program. In addition, many know that one of my special treats is spaghetti, so we had a spaghetti dinner with garlic bread at the end of every program as we shared in the special farewells and good-byes over a steaming platter of Italian goodness.

Food is powerful, and the home-cooked meals exemplified our desire to provide for the emotional and mental healing of the heart and the soul with each program.

> **"I realized very early the power of food**
> **to evoke memory, to bring people together,**
> **to transport you to other places**
> **I wanted to be part of that."**
> —Jose Andreas Puerta

Story and Clark Piano

If pianos could talk, our upright Story and Clark instrument would have hundreds of stories to tell. It was an original piano crafted in 1906 by a master and not made in an assembly line. It weighed about 1,000 pounds and was a rich maple-colored wood, which I'm guessing was mahogany. Grandma Olson was the original player, and the piano was in the family home on the farm of her youth. There were no piano lessons available to her. She taught herself to play that instrument and it brought countless hours of joy to her listeners.

Story goes that when the family home burned down, Grandma enlisted everyone in sight to move the piano near the door. There was no way to get the piano out of the room, but with the group they assembled, and by pouring buckets of water on it, they were able to stop the home fire. The house was lost and needed to be leveled, but, miraculously, the piano survived intact.

Eventually, the piano made it to grandma's home in Jasper, Minnesota, where for years, family would gather around on holidays and sing the traditional family songs: "Irish Lullaby," "Darktown Strutters Ball," "Sentimental Journey," and "You Always Hurt the One You Love." Looking back now, it's interesting to understand the backstories of some of the lyrics. We closed out most gatherings with "Amazing Grace." With the whole family part of the piano's life, there was no way to let it go when Grandma was too old to keep her home.

My family home, a hundred miles away, became the new home of the piano. In grade school, I took some lessons—just enough to play songs for the family get-togethers. In high school, more playing more brought sparks of joy. After I graduated and moved away, the piano went silent unless I was home for a weekend. Learning how to string copper wire between the strings and make it sound like a "honky-tonk" was especially fun. Finally, after a few years of silence, the piano moved in with me. My moves numbered ten, and each one included the piano—including long-distance to Austin, Texas, and Palm Desert, California.

Every move had at least one story. For instance, when we moved from Hopkins, Minnesota, we had sold the house, with three days to go until closing. The movers had trouble with that 1,000 pounds of piano and they lost their grip. The piano tipped and went through the wall of the living room. It cost us the closing and we had to put house back on the market where it took another seven months to sell. Needless to say, after many years, a great deal of moving money, and angst, the time came to sell the piano. It was wrenching to look at the drink rings where many a glass or bottle had sat, or to run your fingers over the scratches from four generations of family, and to set the old sheet music one more time. After months of unsuccessfully trying to sell it and finally trying to give it away, the piano went to "piano heaven." No one else was willing to go to the trouble of moving it.

We all still miss "The Piano." Even though covered with drink stains and cigarette burns, it held generations of history.

"Music gives a soul to the universe, wings to the mind, flight to the imagination and life to everything."
—Plato

Touchstones

It's been said that some experiences and repeated behaviors become touchstones in a person's life. We develop some memories to which we can return, where we can relive some very important times that help shape of our days and the quality of life we have. We are influenced by repeated happenings.

A touchstone in my life has been the Sunday dinners I grew up with as a child. It was always one of three menus. It revolved around beef, chicken, or pork, always roasted in the oven before we went to church and ready to add the sides and salad when we came home. Weeknights, we could have spaghetti, meatloaf, or tuna casserole, but Sunday dinner needed to make itself while we were in church. Driving home from church, each of us knew our jobs. Dad's was making homemade butter and mashing the potatoes; mine was making salads; my mother's was making gravy. My sister was in charge of making dessert or my brother would make ice cream cups.

Everyone got busy as soon as church was over, and the adults had a cocktail or a beer. We gathered around the dining room table, always used the Franciscan Apple pattern dishes, and there would be guests. My uncle Henie was always there, sometimes my grandpa Olson, and a neighbor or two. It was a festive occasion and was followed by me "being busy." I often did the dishes while my parents enjoyed a cigarette and another cocktail. As soon as dishes were done, I played the piano and people would sing. It was the same most every Sunday of high school. Sometimes, others would help with dishes as they wanted to get to the piano playing and singing.

These times are a foundation for me of connection, joy, good food, conversation, belonging, and laughter. That is a touchstone of my life today and, whenever possible, I like to bring parts of that era into my life through family, friends, music, food and laughter. It's all possible once there is a touchstone.

"The tradition of the Sunday dinner accomplishes more than just feeding us. It nurtures us!"
—Chef John Besh

Trust the Process

To follow one's passion contributes to a life well lived. Holding my memory sacred, it fills me with wonder, joy, sometimes regret and pain, but always keeps me fulfilled. As a writer, it's important for me not to know the ending of anything that I write. Writing is an adventure for me and wondering what is going to happen is part of the joy it brings me. It becomes important to have a thought, memory, passion, idea, or conviction and then start writing and see where it goes. Overthinking and overplanning seems to stop the process; learning to "trust the process" has been my magic to success.

My advice it to simply start and go with that process. It seems that there is the visitation in one's mind by unexpected flashes of memory or thoughts that at first seem unrelated to anything else: they just "pop up." My writing style has been to start with that thought and end up someplace else. Writing is my zone and a sea of words come to me. It is like a puzzle that comes together into a picture.

Reading the story of Roger Ebert, as a writer and as a critic, I related to him. We both resisted the idea of social media; simply too time consuming without enough joy and gift. Yet we both appreciate words and use computers to document those words. When writing, the hours fly by. It's 7:30 in the morning and before I know it it's 7:30 at night. In between a walk and a bit of food for my physical self, maybe one phone or Zoom call for my social life, necessary clothes for comfort, and a few prayers always for my spiritual self and maybe read a few chapters in a favorite book, but then the writing starts and pulls it all together. Perhaps for you, the chapters in a book, a TV show, a meal, exercise—we are all different and the world is a place where all can happen, but for me—it's writing that makes my world go round. Find your passion, simply start, and always "trust the process."

**"Trust the process of your life to unfold and know,
without a doubt, that through the highs and lows,
your heart and soul are secure in love
from a power outside yourself!"**
–Sharon Cruse

Scrapbooks and Videos

Scrapbooks have become a bit like books. There is less production as communication and collections go online and are instant. However, for me, scrapbooks will never lose their charm. My father scrapbooked himself through World War II and reading the old news clippings and seeing the gas and chocolate ration books helps me savor the black-and-white photos. He has provided rare historical records. My grandmother gave me an early Brownie camera, and I began to take photos at about eight years old.

My life has been busy with my Brownie camera, film, and later my cameras that used flash bulbs and the disappointment if a bulb didn't flash and everyone would have to line up again. Hundreds of photos, and rolls of film and flashbulbs, later, my collection was saved in paper scrapbooks. Saving both photos and stories of my large Scottish clan of my grandmother's family and being the only one to take and save photos from my French and Belgium dad's family means I have the heritage that, hopefully, will someday be digitized by someone and passed down to future generations.

When my great-granddaughter was born, I wrote a letter to tell her about her seven grandmas for whom there are photos and stories. I asked my grandson to give her that letter when she is twelve years old. Held by me as treasures, the photos of the family history, and pages of family stories are preserved in 100 scrapbooks held in my unit. They are about the family that looked well, but all had underlying stories going on as well.

Additionally, there are also photos and stories from a trip around the world that we experienced a few years ago. Energy comes from these collections of personal history, and I consider them one of my greatest treasures. In recent times, I have digitized many videos and film as well, and it's fulfilling to walk through history and re-experience it all again. Some days, I wonder: did all this history really happen? It's been an enchanted life.

Yes, it did, and I have the recorded proof. How wonderful is that?

"We gather up pictures and bits of our past and scrapbook them into a gift that will last."
—Kimberly Rinehard

Chapter Twelve
Travel

Amphitheater in Red Rocks

There is a famous amphitheater in Morrison, Colorado, called Red Rocks. It is unmatched in its beauty, set in the foothills of the Rocky Mountains, and has perfect acoustics. You can take in a Broadway-type show, concerts of all kinds, and theater. Another is Tuacahn Amphitheatre in Ivins, Utah. Both sites present the beauty of mountains, sky, and fresh air entertainment. The back of the Tuacahn Theaters boasts an open backdrop deep in the canyon and is often pulled right into the drama. Both theaters are stunning and offer a delight to experience. Not much equals a cool summer night in either open air theater, talented actors on stage, state of the art equipment and sound system, and a thermos full of hot chocolate or coffee. Sit back and relax.

My experiences in both of these theaters were memorable. My visit to the Red Rock in Morrison was prompted by my being a fan of Garrison Keillor. His yarns and stories woke up the Minnesota girl inside me and listening to the show, "Prairie Home Companion," was my ritual for many years. The night was perfect. About a third of the way into the show, one of famous Colorado summer storms appeared out of nowhere; the wind started to blow, the raindrops were slight, but steady, the speakers crackled a bit, but then adjusted themselves, and Garrison Keillor kept right on telling stories. Ushers ran around warning people to evacuate the theater, and they began helping the very few who left. The rest of us continued. The orchestra packed up their instruments and one by one left the stage. Garrison Keillor kept the microphone and continued telling those Minnesota stories. The wind howled, the lightening was crackling in the sky, and the wires of the speaker system were swaying in the wind. For another hour, Keillor kept the strong and faithful audience entertained. He never missed a beat, and the majority of the audience never left. After all, we were probably mostly Minnesotans where "men are good looking, women are strong, and all the children were above average."

My second experience was in Ivins, Utah, at the Tuacahn Amphitheater. One of its best features is the open backstage. While action is happening onstage, there can be an authentic campfire and horses grazing in the backdrop, out on the actual ground. The night we were there, the actors included an out- of-control motorcycle off in the distance crashing into a campsite. Viewing a distance chaos, while listening carefully to the actors on the stage, put the scene in a very lifelike and real way long before there were techniques developed to get that same feeling electronically.

Imagine the anxiety of the crowd as that same motorcycle came out of the backdrop and headed toward the edge of the stage. However, it was a runaway and not part of the show. The audience fortunately caught on and the as the motorcycle headed toward the stage and eventually off of it, crashing into the first four rows. What was a special part of the theater became a true life event. The theater promised a lifelike relationship to the actors and the drama. It actually delivered in ways beyond anyone's expectations!

> **"Doesn't expecting the unexpected make the unexpected expected?"**
> —Bob Dylan

Bates Motel to Chateau Marmont

As a conference speaker in the early days, often it was a struggling non-profit group that selected my lodging. Eager to deliver "the message," as some of us younger zealots called it, I would head off and "trust the process." One that stands out in my mind was in Gary, Indiana. My driver, also hired by the agency, looked forlorn as he said, "Here we are!" We looked at each other, and I asked him to stay while I checked in. Of course, he did. They were nice enough, and he brought my bags to my room. It was raining, cold, and very dark. I was not about to deal with my accommodations at that point. From my room, I could hear different gentlemen friends about every two hours on one side and a couple arguing on the other side until daylight came through the windows. Early morning found me packed and ready to go when my driver appeared at my door.

I told my hosts, "Either find me suitable accommodations or my contract is finished. They found better accommodations.

History let me know that some of the same things that went on in the cheap motel in Gary, Indiana went on in better hotels as well. My next week, I was at the Chateau Marmont in Los Angeles, California. Checking in and seeing Natalie Wood also checking in and Liza Minnelli in the lounge gave me a clue this hotel was going to be quite okay. I also discovered Jim Belushi meeting with friends in the lobby. Going to dinner was like a who's who of various celebrities, and my hosts assured me this would be a night to remember. Despite the upscale crowd and accommodations, it was the same presentation, the same "message." When it comes right down to it, people are more alike than different. It's the circumstances and chance that make the difference.

In Austin, Texas, workshops often meant for me to show up in formal gowns and, after a dinner, my hostess would pull out an old green chalkboard and I would get to work. This is the same company that used lavender ink in all ballpoint pens and had small chandeliers in the elevators.

Traveling in all crowds taught me lessons and gave me confidence that if the message was the truth, it touched all kinds of minds, hearts, and souls.

**"Service to others gives life
purpose and meaning."**
—Kamala Harris

**"Expect the unexpected and,
whenever possible,
be the unexpected."**
—Lynda Barry

Black Sand Beaches and Tapatui

Black sand beaches are beautiful and magical. We were in Tahiti and loved to stroll in the warm sand.

Our tour was about twelve people and our guide turned us over to a local dancer. He said he would drive us back to our tour in his van. We enjoyed this dancer who enthralled us all with his moves and special costumes. He was a graceful, sometimes wild, and always entertaining. As the afternoon wore on and I would have thought he was spent, he came and asked my husband if he could ask me to dance.

I left my shoes and went into the sand and did my best to learn many of his moves. It was a delightful experience, and my husband was filming my every move. Finally, the day ended and we all shared fruit drinks, shaved ice, and laughed about our adventures. We felt we had been touched by a true Tahitian native, one who was both authentic and an honest representation of this beautiful country. Up until this time, the only time the dancer had spoken was asking my husband for permission to dance with me.

By the time this dance was performed, he had taken off more and more of his costume and gowns and was left only wearing a thong. Every single inch of his body was covered in tattoos. He explained each of them to us. The ancient beliefs, the history, and the spirit of the island was spoken through his tattoos, and we learned about it all. The dancer introduced himself as "Tapatui."

It was then time to walk back to the path, reclaim our shoes, and head toward his twelve-passenger bus. We were standing in line at the bus as he caught up with us to open the door and stop to kiss our cheeks as we boarded. He had not reclaimed any of his clothes as he stood there in his thong.

He asked us where we were from. Joe answered, "Las Vegas." Tapatui broadened his already huge smile and said, "Las Vegas, Las Vegas, my favorite vacation spot. I love to go to Las Vegas." He then reached into this "barely there" thong and from somewhere pulled out a business card and attempted to hand it to Joe. I saw Joe cringe because no one could imagine in this string thong where that card had been. Tapatui continued, "My favorite casino is the Luxor. I will contact you when I am coming. We shall be together again." This announcement didn't change the magic of the black sand beaches, but it gave us more to think about. We have never forgotten Tahiti and Tapatui!

"We get together because of similarities, but we grow with difference. Don't miss any encounters because there are often surprises."
—Sharon Cruse

"One cannot plan for the unexpected."
—Aaron Klug

The Golden Gate Bridge

Driving across the Golden Gate Bridge was daunting for a small-town Minnesota girl who was used to local roads, where the widest highways were a hundred miles away in Minneapolis. Flying into Los Gatos and renting a car was the beginning of my love affair with California. First it was coast road, in search of lunch at Nepenthe, with open pit patio dining, in Big Sur and then continuing to Esalen by late afternoon check in. The road came complete with closures, rockslides, and twisting curves. The car felt like it was hugging the road and the ocean lapped precariously below. The road always felt dangerous, and it was good to check in and know the trip home meant the car could hug the coast instead of a guard rail. I took over fourteen trips to Esalen over the years, and the road became familiar, but never easy.

By the time I was ready for a San Francisco adventure, driving in California traffic was getting much heavier than in the 1970s going to Esalen. My work in San Francisco was finished, and it was time for me to travel to Sausalito, just across the Golden Gate Bridge. I had a friend with me, and we were eager for the trip. We started out from the San Francisco side and were sailing along, singing to great music, and then the car started to sputter, then sputter more, until we slowly pulled over to the side the best we could and came to a stop. We didn't have car trouble; we were simply out of gas. I couldn't believe I let that happen. Traffic had a hard time getting around us and it wasn't long before a police car was right there. My first thought was *Great, we have help!* I was wrong, as I soon discovered. As I learned, it was illegal to not take responsibility for your car on the bridge. Not having enough gas in your tank fell into that category. We were arrested and taken in the police car to Sausalito to pay a hefty fine then were driven back to the car with a very expensive can of gas and a stern warning. We made it across the bridge and continued on our way.

About two weeks later, I received the ticket in the mail, and they had changed it to a "warning" about responsibility. No fine. Once I felt relief, the memory of sitting behind the plastic barrier, riding in the police car, going before the powers that be and feeling like a criminal were not feelings I enjoyed whatsoever. I didn't tell them that I had my camera with me and forever have the photo of my friend and I riding in the back of a police car.

"The cover-up, more than the initial wrongdoing, is what is most likely to bring you down."
—Madeline Albright

Meetings in New York

In the mid 1970s, powerhouse Mona Mansell called and said, "You must come to New York. I am going to start a center that will recognize the family dysfunction of alcoholism. You must come." Mona had been part of my training programs in Minneapolis at the Johnson Institute. She learned "Families don't have to wait for a crisis to intervene in addiction. No one needs to hit bottom to get help. Knowledge and intervention methods can raise that bottom and a change in behavior could come much sooner." Now she wanted to start her own institute, the Freedom Institute, to be headquartered in New York, New York. Frank Sinatra said, "If you can make it here, you can make it anywhere," so, of course, I said "Yes, tell me when and where." That was the first of many trips to New York to stay in Mona and Frank's apartment.

It was a long way from a farming community to board meetings in New York. Learning the commute to the city, the taxi system, how to have intimate family meetings with movers and shakers was a challenge, but I was ready for it and the institute was born. Anytime and anywhere alcoholic families were on the agenda, my intent was to help make it happen.

Working in a corporate system from the top down is very different than working from the bottom up. As always, my policy was to start at the top of a business or a family system and listen to what is happening at that level. It's then very simple to design programs, find funding, and to follow through on help "that really works." Given that chance in New York by Mona Mansell and being able to do interventions into addicted families and employees made a difference in those early days of family treatment. We were able to start at the top of many companies and corporations. We had already worked with that private group in Minnesota. A friend taught me that wealthy and powerful families hurt in the same way as poor families do—in their hearts and souls.

A bonus was the chance to learn about some of the best delis (to this day, some of my favorite food), to learn to handle the taxi service of a city like New York (yellow cabs in my day), walking through Central Park to dine at the historic Tavern on the Green, and even to listen to sirens every night. These were wonderful days, and all made possible by the vision of a great female icon, Mona Mansell.

> **"There is something in the New York air**
> **that makes sleep useless."**
> —Simone de Beauvoir

Don't Do as the Romans Do?

Joe and I enjoyed a romantic interlude dining outside at the Via Appia in Rome. There was candlelight, music in the background, and the very best pizza ever. It was a slice of heaven.

After we were seated, the waiter asked us for our wine order. All visitors to Rome learn the wines, the choices, and make the selection. Red and white of some kind was being offered in many tastings and I did all the tasting, which seemed to bother the waiter a bit in this very male atmosphere. However, I continued to taste and then selected a glass. He stared at both of us and said, "Bottle only." Joe then proceeded to order a soda. The waiter looked again, a bit taken back and shocked.

Joe spoke a combination (his own) of Spanish and Italian. He launched, as only Joe could do, into his story of recovery from alcohol many years ago and did his best to help the waiter understand that he didn't drink wine. When you are an Italian waiter in an upscale Roman restaurant, this is a hard concept to understand. He was patient and so was Joe and they laughed and gestured and, finally, after a long time, he brought me a glass of wine and served the pizza. It was a grand night and one we talked about for years.

Several years later, after many trips and many adventures, we wanted to go to Rome again. It was one of our favorite destinations. We love staying at the Villa de Peppo. (Side story: I had my favorite throw pillow at this hotel and Joe simply bought it from the manager upon checking out. It still is beside my bed). Perhaps this hotel has changed many names by now. Back to Via Appia. We decided to visit this quaint restaurant and order another pizza. As we were seated, I noticed the same waiter was still there. We were going to tell him about our previous visit. No need. He saw us come in and was soon at our table with my favorite wine bottle—bottle, not glass. He looked at Joe and shook his head, "No" and smiled. He brought Joe a soda. The two picked up like old buddies. We never forgot him and, apparently, he didn't forget us or Joe's story.

Needless to say, the whole meal was a gift from the restaurant to both Joe and I along with a special look that went between Joe and the waiter.

I will always want to visit the Via Appia Restaurant when in Rome. This is one time that the old saying, "When in Rome, do as the Romans do," didn't work that way. Joe did what he wanted to do, and no one ever forgot it.

**"Everyone, sooner or later,
comes round by Rome."**
—Robert Browning

The Trip of a Lifetime—Intimacy

Whenever Joe and I would come to a conflict—one would want one thing, the other would want something else—we made the decision to find a way to "do both." Most of the time, we could find the way. Sometimes we couldn't, but those times were rare if we really studied the situation. If it was something simple, like dinner, we could do two nights' dinner, and each have our own way. If it was buying a car, we could each give up our idea and find a third solution we could agree on. If it was a television show, watch one and tape the other.

The biggest, of course, was where will we vacation, and that was the idea behind our trip around the world and which solved that issue for years to come.

We learned the lesson that the reason we loved each other so deeply is we were each attracted to the other to complete what we already knew and loved. The partner filled in the missing blanks. It was clear in our relationship how that worked. Joe loved golf. I didn't. No matter how hard I tried, the game bored me. So, he played golf and I had time to do the things that interested me. I was crazy about loud Jerry Lee Lewis music whenever I did household chores. He went out to coffee with his friends when the house rocked with music. I would have never known about "doctor stories" without Joe, and he would have never known about rock and roll without me. The scientist and the hippie each found their way and it was a collision of souls.

What mattered and what counts, and that is perhaps true for all, is: how one feels about family (past, current, and future); how one feels about money, security and safety; how one feels spiritually. These are what bring people together. How they are willing to communicate these feelings determine the quality of the relationship and what one gives and takes from being together. When those values connect, there is magic.

We took the trip of our life on a world cruise: three months; thirty-seven countries; the same table for two with candlelight by a window; daily lunch with friends. Elephants, camels, costumes, new friends, old history and a private balcony overlooking the ocean. Intimacy, fear, and excitement were all part of the magical trip of a lifetime.

"Every choice you make has consequences, certain losses, certain gains, possible losses and possible gains. Decide if the possible gains are worth the certain losses and if they are, find the courage to leap. If they aren't, make peace with and appreciate the choice not to risk what you already have."
—Joe Zantomata

"Storytelling is our obligation
to the next generation."
—Laura Holloway

Study Guide

It is my hope that you enjoyed the stories I've shared in this book, and that they sparked some ideas for you to consider and ways for you to tell some of your own stories. The study guide might help you to do this, or perhaps you have your own style. Just wake up to your storyteller inside and keep those memories alive long after life dances through chance.

Storytelling imparts wisdom, brings a smile or a tear, and builds bridges. Give those you love a sense of the meaning of your life. Your legacy of stories will long outlive you. We all have them. Join the adventure and relish the outcome.

> **"It is not that I live in the past,**
> **it's that the past lives in me."**
> —Mary Antin

Telling stories to each other unlocks deep feelings and the long-ago memories contained within them. They help us connect and foster intimacy. We are our stories.

Carefully choose about eight or ten people to become part of your group. This guide is set up for ten sharing sessions. You can either meet weekly or monthly. Choose a general topic for that session. Decide on a schedule and the maximum time for each person to share. Then, add in time for an opening and closing. Select someone to be the timekeeper—the one who makes sure each person stays within their time limit. It's good to have a timer set, with sound, because then it is clear that time is up for that person's contribution. If a story runs over the time limit, the timer simply says, "Bookmark it for next time" and move on. The storyteller saves the rest of the story for the next time.

What Is the Purpose of the Group?

The purpose of the group is to provide each person a time to share an event, whether from the recent past or something that happened long ago. The story needs to have a beginning, a middle, and an end. The storyteller should share the main point of the story, and then each member will share if they got the same point or maybe add others that they thought of or felt. The group sharing will then transition into each person sharing their personal story on the topic chosen for that session. The guide below will facilitate this process.

After each person has told their story for that session, the guide will summarize what had been said, reminding the group of the topic for the next session so members can be thinking in advance, and then group is adjourned.

Understanding the Group Gathering

The guide invites eight to ten people to join a "story sharing" or "story vision" group.

The role of the guide is to facilitate the process of group sharing and set the ground rules for each session. Here are some basics for setting up the group.

1. Who is the guide and why has this group been chosen?

2. How long should our sessions be? Two hours is a suggested time.

3. Choose a ten-session timeframe. For instance, every Sunday afternoon from 2:00 to 4:00, or the first Saturday morning of the month from 10:00 to noon.

4. Decide on a convenient and comfortable location for the group to meet.

5. Set ground rules of sharing when group is over. Many people are more eager to share if they know that what is said in the room will stay in the room and not repeated to others.

Session One Format

The facilitator guides the setup of the group, as noted above. The facilitator follows these steps:

1. Ask the individuals in attendance, "Do you want to commit to the ten-session group?

2. To make sure everyone is on board with the program, ask, "Do you like telling and hearing stories?"

3. Ask, "What is a story from your life that you like and enjoy?

4. Pass out the ten-topic sessions to plan in advance.

5. Make sure to set a policy of no stories about health, politics, or religion.

The Ten Story Topics

1. Traditions
2. Travel
3. Culture or history
4. Life lessons
5. Surprises
6. Friends
7. Humor
8. People
9. Values
10. Family or relationships

About the
Author

Sharon Wegscheider-Cruse is a family therapist, businesswoman, and founder of Onsite Workshops. She is the author of twenty-three books, including five bestsellers, translated into thirteen languages, most notably *Another Chance: Hope and Health for the Alcoholic Family, Learning to Love Yourself, Choicemaking,* and *Caregiving: Hope and Health for Caregiving Families..*

She has brought hope and healing to millions through her company, Onsite Workshops, TN, and fostered a movement that brought direction to millions of adult children of alcoholics. The co-founder of the National Association of Children of Alcoholics (NACOA), she has trained and lectured for the US Air Force, counseling agencies, spa wellness centers, and corporations. She has developed programs in the United States, Europe, Canada, Australia, and New Zealand.

Sharon has appeared on numerous television and radio shows, including *The Oprah Winfrey Show, The Phil Donahue Show, The Larry King Show,* and *The Today Show.*

Her love for her soulmate, Joe, is everlasting and her greatest accomplishment is her joy for her children, her grandchildren, and relationships with her friends.

For more information about Sharon and her work, or to contact her, please visit her website: *sharonwegscheidercruse.com.*